P9-CAF-617

Abortion

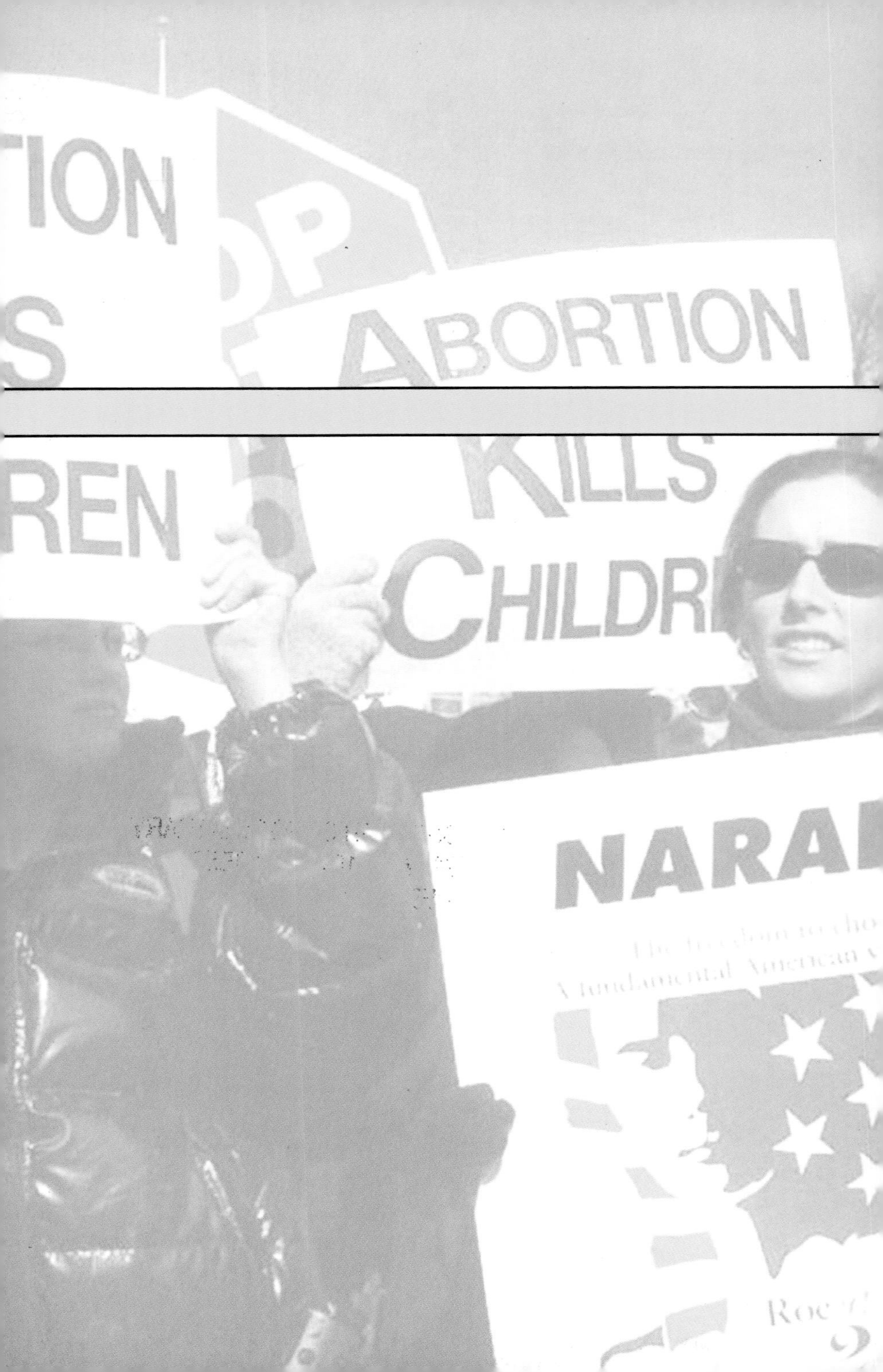
ABORTION
KILLS

I'm pro-choice
and I pray.

Open for Debate

Abortion

Corinne J. Naden

REDMOND HIGH SCHOOL LIBRARY
17272 NE 104TH STREET
REDMOND, WA 98052

NARAL

Marshall Cavendish
Benchmark
New York

Marshall Cavendish Benchmark
99 White Plains Road
Tarrytown, NY 10591
www.marshallcavendish.us
Copyright © 2008 by Marshall Cavendish Corporation

All rights reserved. No part of this book may be reproduced or utilized in any form
or by any means electronic or mechanical including photocopying, recording, or by any
information storage and retrieval system, without permission from the copyright holders.

All Internet sites were available and accurate when sent to press.

Library of Congress Cataloging-in-Publication Data
Naden, Corinne J.
Abortion / by Corinne J. Naden.
p. cm. — (Open for debate)
Summary: "Presents all sides of the abortion debate and includes a discussion
of the medical rights associated with abortion and the history and politics
affecting this debate in America"—Provided by publisher.
Includes bibliographical references and index.
ISBN-13: 978-0-7614-2573-1
1. Abortion—Law and legislation—United States—Juvenile literature.
2. Abortion—United States—Juvenile literature. I. Title. II. Series.
KF3771.Z9N33 2007
342.7308'4—dc22 2006028525

Photo research by Lindsay Aveilhe and Linda Sykes/
Linda Sykes Picture Research, Inc., Hilton Head, SC

AP/Wide World Photos: cover, 6; The Granger Collection: 15;
Bettmann/Corbis: 17; © Robert Estall/Corbis: 23;
AP/Wide World Photos, Inc.: 27, 35, 55, 65, 73, 108; -epa/Corbis: 39;
Steve Starr/Corbis: 47; Sophie Elbaz/Corbis Sygma: 58;
D. Tulis/Atlanta Constitution/Corbis Sygma: 81; Wally McNamee/Corbis: 83;
Time & Life Pictures/Getty Images: 89; Charles W. Luzler/Reuters/Corbis: 97;
Jason Reed/ Reuters/Corbis: 112.

Publisher: Michelle Bisson
Art Director: Anahid Hamparian
Series Designer: Sonia Chaghatzbanian

Printed in China

1 3 5 6 4 2

Contents

ABORTION KILLS CHILDREN

ABORTION KILLS CHILDREN

NARAL

The freedom to choose:
A fundamental American value

Roe v. Wade
25th
Anniversary

Foreword

On January 22, 1973, the United States Supreme Court decided that a woman had a legal right to an abortion. The case was *Roe* v. *Wade*, and the vote was 7 to 2. That decision has become one of the most controversial ever issued by the Court. Americans who feel strongly on either side of the issue are divided into two camps. They are generally known as pro-life and pro-choice.

On March 6, 2006, South Dakota became the latest U.S. state to challenge *Roe* v. *Wade*. In the years following the Court decision, there have been other attempts to eat away at the abortion law, such as laws passed in Rhode Island in 1973 and in Louisiana and Utah in 1991. The law in South Dakota makes it a crime for a doctor to perform an abortion in the state even in cases of rape or incest.

South Dakota is already one of the most difficult states in which to get an abortion. It has only one abortion clinic. The Planned Parenthood clinic in Sioux Falls schedules abortions once a week. About eight hundred are performed each year by four visiting doctors. They fly in from Minnesota on a rotating basis. South Dakota's doctors have been reluctant to perform abortions because of the antiabortion sentiment in the state.

Where Americans Stand

A national Harris telephone poll conducted in March 2005 collected information concerning where adult Americans stand on abortion. These are some of the results:

60% favor legal abortion in the first trimester of pregnancy
72% oppose it in the second trimester and 86% in the third
55% support legal abortion in some but not all circumstances
52% support *Roe* v. *Wade*
42% favor no change in the law
42% favor laws that make it more difficult to obtain an abortion
23% favor legal abortion in all circumstances
21% oppose legal abortion in all circumstances

As soon as the new ban was announced, the opposing side voiced its opinion. Kate Looby, state director of Planned Parenthood, which is challenging the law, charged Governor Mike Rounds with caring "more about politics than about the reproductive freedom of women in South Dakota." The republican governor signed the bill into law. Looby called it distressing that "this legislative body cares so little about women, about families, about women who are victims of rape or incest."

Troy Newman, of the Kansas antiabortion group Operation Rescue, called the ban "a grassroots movement that is propelling the legislatures . . . to nullify the permissive abortion laws." Supporters hoped the new law would lead to a direct challenge to *Roe* v. *Wade*, which ruled that state governments had no power to prohibit abortions. However, in November 2006, South Dakota voters rejected the ban by a vote of 56 to 44 percent.

Similar bans on abortion have been introduced in Georgia, Indiana, Kentucky, Ohio, and Tennessee, although those bills did not pass, either. Some opponents of abortion have become more confident of change since conservatives John G. Roberts Jr. and Samuel A. Alito Jr. were appointed to the Court by President George W. Bush in late 2005 and early 2006, respectively.

This is not the first time that South Dakota has placed restrictions on abortion. In 2005, it passed five abortion laws. One says that doctors must tell the woman that she is about to end the life of a "whole, separate, unique human being." Planned Parenthood has a lawsuit on file against it.

Although the South Dakota law went into effect on July 1, 2006, a federal judge suspended it during the course of the legal challenge. Whether in that state or elsewhere, it is likely that the debate over an issue that affects and divides many Americans will continue.

The History of Abortion

A human pregnancy generally lasts nine months, divided into three trimesters, or periods of three months each. There are two types of abortions: spontaneous and induced. A spontaneous abortion is also called a miscarriage. If it occurs later than the first trimester, it may be called a preterm birth. It may occur because something is wrong with the embryo (this is called a genetic abnormality), or it may be due to some kind of trauma such as an auto accident.

An induced abortion is performed for a purpose at any gestational age. It may be done to save the life or mental health of the mother. For instance, after becoming pregnant, a woman may discover that she is suffering from a disease that might result in her death if the pregnancy continues. An induced abortion may stop a pregnancy that resulted from rape or incest. Abortions also may be performed when it is known that the child will have a serious physical or mental deformity. Most induced abortions result from social or economic reasons that make women unwilling to continue pregnancies. Extreme poverty, for instance, may make a woman decide to end a pregnancy.

In the first trimester, or first three months, the medical procedure known as abortion removes the embryo from the uterus before it has reached what is called the stage of viability, which begins at the twenty-fourth week of the pregnancy. Before that time the embryo cannot survive on its own outside the uterus. An abortion is performed under local anesthetic. A small, hollow suction tube removes the embryo. The procedure takes about ten minutes. If the abortion occurs later than three months into the pregnancy, an operation is required to remove the fetus (the term generally used past the first trimester).

There has long been controversy over whether and when abortions should be performed and the extent to which they should be encouraged or denied. The issue has divided religious and political leaders. It has involved the old and the young. It enrages those who oppose it on religious grounds. It enrages those who defy any restriction on a woman's right to her own body and to making decisions about her own complex life circumstances.

In Early America

Birth control and abortion were at times and under certain circumstances acceptable even back in the Greco-Roman world. That is true in Jewish and Christian theology as well. However, abortions were very dangerous. Through the centuries, abortion methods have included drinking various herb concoctions and stabbing the womb with a sharp object. Indeed, abortions often did result from such practices. So did physical harm to, or even the death of, the woman.

Under English law in the Middle Ages, pregnancy was said to begin at quickening, when the woman first felt movement from the fetus. The law did not recognize a woman as being pregnant before that time, so ending the pregnancy was not a crime. In *Beyond Choice*, Alexander Sanger quotes Justice Harry Blackmun in the *Roe v. Wade* decision: "makes it now appear doubtful that abortion was ever firmly established as a common-law crime even with respect to the destruction of a quick fetus."

Following English law, abortion was legal at least to quickening in colonial America as well. However, there was little public discussion of the reproductive process or control of it. Abortions were publicly condemned both by the legal authorities and by the church. To the colonial Puritans, abortion was a sin.

By the nineteenth century, medical advances made abortions somewhat safer and more were performed. More states passed laws against them. In 1829, for instance, New York banned anyone, including doctors, from attempting an abortion at any time except to save the life of the woman. Well into the 1800s, more and more states passed some kind of restriction on abortions. The woman who had one was considered a criminal in Kentucky, New Jersey, Oregon, South Carolina, and Texas.

Medical conditions improved, but abortion was still dangerous. Some argued that laws prohibiting abortions were passed to protect the health of women. However, as noted by R. Sauer in an article in *Population Studies* entitled "Attitudes to Abortion in America, 1800–1973": "In the minds of many, safeguarding the mother's health was held to be secondary to the protection of the foetus as a rationale for anti-abortion laws; many valued foetal life highly in itself and felt that this life should be protected by law."

As a result of all these laws and the general confusion over the issue, abortions were still performed but under greater and greater secrecy. Women faced great difficulty and danger in obtaining one and usually paid a very high price for it. That condition would last well into the 1900s.

The passage of laws that restricted a woman's right to an abortion tied in with the image of women at the time. Women were increasing their numbers in the work force, which many men regarded as a threat to their own work status. A working woman went against the idea of her prime role as producing and caring for children. The American Medical Association (AMA) strengthened this view when it issued a report in 1871 stating that an abortion went against the true purpose of a woman's life.

The passage of the 1873 federal Comstock Act also reflected this attitude about the role of women. Legally, it was known as the Act for the Suppression of Trade in, and Circulation of, Obscene Literature and Articles of Immoral Use. It was the result of strong lobbying by Anthony Comstock (1844–1915), self-appointed keeper of the nation's morals. For some forty years this zealous reformer crusaded against what he considered to be obscenity in literature, even the classics. He was especially against people he called libertines, meaning those who were somewhat free in their sexual conduct. It is said that he bragged about how many of them he caused to commit suicide.

The Comstock Act had five sections, the last forbidding obscene materials to be sent through the mail. That included anything that was intended to prevent conception or induce abortion. Those convicted could spend up to ten years at hard labor and/or pay a fine of up to five thousand dollars.

It is worth noting that abortion, as with other major social issues, has been affected by the climate of the times. In the 1800s when many restrictive laws against abortion were passed, many men, and women as well, believed that the primary role of a woman was to become a mother. In 1973 when *Roe* v. *Wade* was passed, times had changed.

Abortion was already legal in much of the developed world, including predominantly Catholic Italy.

Into the Twentieth Century

In the early 1900s, an obstetrics nurse in New York City grew more and more disturbed by the high death rate from illegal, botched abortions. Margaret Sanger (1879–1966) went on to lead the birth control movement in the United States. She believed that every woman had a right to avoid an unwanted pregnancy. She also advocated other controversial stands, such as her belief that marriage should not include the right to parenthood or that the unfit should have fewer children. Sanger opened her first birth control clinic in Brooklyn, New York, in 1916, and was promptly arrested.

Many more arrests followed, so many that public opinion began to turn in Sanger's favor because the suffering that resulted from illegal abortions was well known. Through her work and mounting pressure from other groups, the federal courts finally allowed doctors to give advice about birth control methods. And in 1936 the Comstock Law was reinterpreted. Doctors could now import and distribute contraceptives to avoid pregnancies.

Sanger founded the National Birth Control League in 1916, renamed the American Birth Control League in 1921. In 1942, it became part of the Planned Parenthood Federation of America. By 1960, birth control was legal in forty-eight states. Sanger also took her birth control campaign to foreign countries such as Japan and India.

As in the United States, most countries have a varied history on the subject of abortion. Chinese folklore says Emperor Shennong spoke of using mercury to induce abortions about five thousand years ago. Greek physician Soranus details how to induce abortions in his second-

MARGARET SANGER WAS *THE* PIONEER IN THE BIRTH CONTROL MOVEMENT IN THE UNITED STATES IN THE EARLY TWENTIETH CENTURY. THIS 1918 CARTOON IN HER PERIODICAL, *BIRTH CONTROL REVIEW*, EXPRESSES HER STANDPOINT ON THE ISSUE.

century text *Gynecology.* Documents dating from the twelfth century in Japan discuss how to bring on an abortion. The British Parliament passed a law outlawing abortion in 1861 and legalized it in limited cases in 1967. Pope Pius IX declared the procedure gravely immoral in 1869. Vladimir Lenin, leader of the Soviet Union, legalized all abortions in 1920. Joseph Stalin reversed that in 1936 in order to increase the population. In the late 1960s and 1970s, abortion became legal throughout the developed world, and *Roe* v. *Wade* became part of that happening. In the late twentieth century, China actually promoted the use of abortions on a large scale to control its population growth.

The Court Considers
Roe v. *Wade*

In the last half of the twentieth century, the idea surfaced in the United States that a woman might have a constitutional right to sexual privacy and freedom. This idea went against the view that a woman was destined for her main role as a mother.

Abortion was illegal in the United States except to save the woman's life in the 1960s. There were all sorts of restrictions, such as therapeutic abortion committees, which were designated groups of doctors in hospitals that decided on the viability of abortions. There was also inequitable access to abortions, meaning that in some instances the wealthy found the means to an abortion while others could not. But in 1962 the Model Penal Code of the American Law Institute (ALI) recommended that the procedure be legal in certain circumstances, such as a pregnancy resulting from a rape. Some of the states began to adopt ALI recommendations, and Alaska, Hawaii, and New York repealed their abortion laws.

In 1965, the Supreme Court, in *Griswold* v. *Connecticut*, struck down a law that made it a crime to use any drug, article, or instrument to prevent conception. The statute had been in force in Connecticut since 1879 and had been challenged twice before. The suit was filed by two members of the state's Planned Parenthood Federation. They had been convicted for giving medical advice and instruction to married couples about contraception.

In *Abortion and American Politics*, Barbara Craig and David O'Brien say that the 7 to 2 decision of the Court "established a constitutional right to a realm of privacy. The Court ruled that the right to use contraceptives lay with a protected 'zone of privacy' . . . emanating from several provisions of the Bill of Rights." The case caused little

Estelle Griswold (L), medical advisor and executive director of the Planned Parenthood clinic in New Haven, CT, and Cornelia Jahncke, president of the Parenthood League of Connecticut, Inc., flash a victory sign in response to winning *Griswold* v. *Connecticut*. The Supreme Court rule made contraception legal in Connecticut—in 1965!

public interest at the time, but the privacy issue was important. It would have great impact on later Court decisions, especially *Roe v. Wade*.

Roe v. Wade was argued on December 13, 1971, reargued on October 11, 1972, and decided on January 22, 1973. That decision, one of the Court's most controversial, had a deep impact on the lives of many American women.

The Jane Roe in *Roe v. Wade* was actually Norma McCorvey, a twenty-one-year-old divorcée living in Texas. A high school dropout, she already had a five-year-old daughter. The Wade was Henry Wade, Dallas County

The 1973 Decision

Date: Monday, January 22, 1973
Place: Washington, D.C.
Plaintiff: Norma McCorvey, alias Jane Roe
Defendant: Henry B. Wade, Dallas County district attorney
Claim: Texas abortion law is in violation of McCorvey's and other women's constitutional rights
Plaintiff's lawyers: Sarah Weddington, Linda Coffee
Defendant's lawyers: John Tolle, Jay Floyd, Robert Flowers
Decision: All state laws restricting access to abortion are invalid in first trimester.
Justices: Majority votes—Harry Blackmun, William J. Brennan, Chief Justice Warren Burger, William O. Douglas, Thurgood Marshall, Lewis Powell. Dissenting votes—William Rehnquist, Byron White.

prosecutor. When McCorvey became pregnant in 1969, she could not have an abortion in the state and had no money to go elsewhere for one. She was not politically active or a member of any women's organization. Her case was taken to court too late for her to get an abortion. After her child was adopted, two young lawyers, Sarah Weddington and Linda Coffee, took her case. They were both graduates of the University of Texas Law School and were deeply interested in women's issues.

Roe v. *Wade* reflected what was happening at the time. During the so-called sexual revolution of the 1950s and 1960s, a broad social movement called for relaxing the country's strict antiabortion laws. At the same time, a growing women's movement made those laws a high priority for change. Thalidomide, a drug used to curb morning sickness in pregnant women, was found to occasionally cause severe birth defects. These and other factors began to stir the public. Fourteen states enacted abortion reform laws between 1967 and 1970. Two states rejected abortion legalization votes in the November 1972 elections.

The aim of the young lawyers was to challenge the constitutionality of the Texas law against abortion, which had been adopted in 1854. It said no one could perform an abortion in the state except to save the life of the woman. To challenge the law, McCorvey's lawyers needed a plaintiff just like her, someone who had been forced to do something against her will as a result of the Texas law. They also planned to build on the right-of-privacy issue that had surfaced in *Griswold* v. *Connecticut*. They hoped to get past the federal district court and on to the Supreme Court.

A three-panel court for the Northern Division of Texas, located in Dallas, heard the case and came to a decision on June 17, 1970. The court said that the Texas law

REDMOND HIGH SCHOOL LIBRARY

did infringe on the right of single women and married people to decide whether or not to have children. But the judges did not stop enforcement of the Texas law. Because the case had been heard by a three-judge panel instead of the typical single district court judge, Weddington and Coffee could appeal directly to the Supreme Court. They did so, even though they had never before taken a case to such a level. They were granted a review on May 3, 1971.

The lawyers for McCorvey argued that people have a right to privacy, granted under the Fourteenth Amendment to the U.S. Constitution. The government should not be able to intervene in a private decision such as an abortion.

The lawyers for Wade argued that abortion was murder. McCorvey's life was not in danger because of the pregnancy, they said. They argued that had she been granted an abortion, a human being would have died.

As with all cases before the Supreme Court, after the arguments were presented, the justices met privately to review the points and then to vote. The justices all realized that this was a highly emotional issue. After some delay, Chief Justice Burger decided that the Court was too divided to obtain a majority opinion, meaning that the majority of the Court would be in accord, which would become the basis of law. So, he asked Justice Blackmun to write an opinion, after which the justices would vote. However, after Blackmun presented his opinion, there was still much disagreement and it was decided to reargue the case in the fall.

The case was heard again on October 11, 1972. The Court's 7 to 2 decision was announced on January 23, 1973. According to Kermit Hall in *The Oxford Companion to the Supreme Court of the United States*, the majority of the justices found: "the [Texas] statutes unconstitutional on the ground that they violated the woman's right to privacy, which the opinion located in the Due

Fourteenth Amendment to the U.S. Constitution

Section 1. All persons born or naturalized in the United States, and subject to the jurisdiction thereof, are citizens of the United States and of the state wherein they reside. No state shall make or enforce any law which shall abridge the privileges or immunities of citizens of the United States; nor shall any state deprive any person of the life, liberty, or property, without due process of law; nor deny to any person within its jurisdiction the equal protection of the laws.

Process Clause of the Fourteenth Amendment." In addition, the opinion varied according to the stage of the pregnancy. A woman and her doctor were free to decide on an abortion during the first trimester. An abortion was allowed during the second trimester, although the state could pass laws to protect the health of the woman during this period. Only in the third trimester, said the Court, could the state ban abortions unless having one would save a woman's life. The judges decided that the privacy right in the U. S. Constitution protected a woman's personal decision concerning an abortion.

The dissenting judges in the 7 to 2 decision—Byron White and William Rehnquist (who joined the Court as an associate justice in 1972 and replaced Burger as chief justice in 1986)—argued that the Court was enforcing a right not specified in the Constitution. White said that nothing in the Constitution supported the majority vote.

As noted in Janet Hadley's *Abortion: Between Freedom and Necessity*, in part the Court opinion stated:

The judges of the Supreme Court declared that the "right of privacy" in the United States Constitution is not only fundamental but is also broad enough to protect the personal decision of whether or not to seek an abortion (or use contraception).

A state criminal abortion statute of the current Texas type, that excepts from criminality only a life-saving procedure on behalf of the mother, without regard to pregnancy stage and without recognition of the other interests involved, is violative of the Due Process Clause of the Fourteenth Amendment.

As soon as the decision was announced, reaction was intense and divided. *Roe* v. *Wade* became the rallying cry

CONTRACEPTION COMES, LITERALLY, IN MANY SHAPES AND SIZES. THIS ILLUSTRATION SHOWS A VARIETY OF CONTRACEPTIVE COILS IN USE IN THE UNITED KINGDOM IN THE EARLY 1960S.

of antiabortion factions. Advocacy groups were immediately formed. Federal and state legislators hurried to get their opinions into print. Few knew the far-reaching consequences of that most important decision.

Roe v. *Wade* has been the law for decades. Abortion still causes great controversy in the United States. Those who are against *Roe* v. *Wade* want the decision overturned. Many who favor it cite state laws that may restrict a poor woman's access to abortion. Others feel that restrictions on an adolescent's access, such as requiring a parent's consent, are unfair and harmful. Many pro-choice people fear that allowing state bans on abortion, such as the over-

The Crossing-Over Ministry

In 1995, Norma McCorvey, center of the *Roe* v. *Wade* decision in 1973, became a born-again Christian. She moved from the abortion clinic where she had been working to the national offices of the pro-life Operation Rescue. In 1997, she broke her ties with Operation Rescue and founded the Roe No More Ministry, later renaming it the Crossing-Over Ministry. She completed her autobiography in 1998, entitled *Won by Love*. In June 2003, she filed suit to overturn *Roe* v. *Wade*, but the suit was dismissed because too much time had passed since the original controversy.

McCorvey, now a member of the Roman Catholic Church, frequently talks on TV about her involvement in *Roe* v. *Wade* and her experience in the abortion clinics. When critics question her now anti-*Roe* stance, she replies: "I'm being true to myself and that is all that matters to me and God."*

*Official Press Biography of Norma L. McCorvey

turned law in South Dakota, will push the Court toward overturning *Roe v. Wade*. Pro-lifers hope that by passing more and more restrictions in the states, the Court will eventually have to face the abortion question once again.

Times change, the mood of the country changes, even the Supreme Court changes. It may or may not be a very long time before the Court must once again take up the issue of abortion in the United States. In the meantime, for many Americans the subject is still open for debate.

2
The Issues:
Pro-Choice vs. Pro-Life

Since 1973, abortions have been legal in the United States. With some restrictions that vary by state, a woman can obtain an abortion if she so chooses. Those who agree with the law call themselves pro-choice. They believe that abortion should be a legal option for a woman with an unwanted pregnancy. They believe that a woman should control her own fertility. They do not believe that the government should regulate abortions except where matters of safety and health are concerned.

Those who disagree with the *Roe* v. *Wade* decision call themselves pro-life. They say that abortion is a moral wrong because it causes the death of a human being. They believe that in almost all cases, abortion should be illegal. Pro-life advocates are generally also against stem cell research, which may destroy embryos, and other issues that, for them, touch on the sanctity of life.

When Life Begins

The major difference between pro-choice and pro-life advocates is the question of when life begins, or when the embryo/fetus becomes a person. Their arguments proceed from this issue. For many, it is a religious question. Scientifically, we know that human life, or the life of any mammal, begins at conception, when the sperm fertilizes the egg and the gametes (DNA) fuse. But the questions that separate the views of pro-life and pro-choice are: when does that fusion of sperm and egg become a person, or when does the state protect the human being in the law?

RICHARD H. BLACK, R-LOUDOUN (VA), HOLDS UP PLASTIC MODELS
OF TWELVE-WEEK AND TWENTY-WEEK-OLD FETUSES DURING A 2005
DEBATE ON THE FLOOR OF THE HOUSE OF DELEGATES IN VIRGINIA
ON A BILL THAT WOULD REQUIRE ANESTHESIA TO BE ADMINISTERED
DURING ABORTIONS.

Mission of the Planned Parenthood Federation of America

The National Birth Control League was founded in 1916 under the leadership of Mary Ware Dennett and renamed the American Birth Control League by birth control advocate Margaret Sanger. It became the Planned Parenthood Federation of America, Inc. (PPFA) in 1942. It operates through nationwide health centers, providing health care and information to men, women, and teens. The services vary, including providing prenatal care, contraceptives, a range of gynecological services, and, in some cases, abortions.

"Planned Parenthood believes in the fundamental right of each individual, throughout the world, to manage his or her fertility regardless of the individual's income, marital status, race, ethnicity, sexual orientation, age, national origin, or residence."*

*Planned Parenthood Federation of America
mission statement*

Mission of the National Right to Life Committee

Founded in Detroit in June 1973 after the *Roe* v. *Wade* decision, the National Right to Life Committee (NRLC) now includes more than three thousand chapters in all fifty states. The NRLC also publishes a monthly newspaper, *National Right to Life News*.

The goal of the NRLC is to "restore legal protection to innocent human life."* Although its efforts focus mainly on abortion, it deals with other issues, such as infanticide and euthanasia. It takes no stand on sex education or contraception.

*National Right to Life mission statement

Pro-life advocates believe that life begins at conception. Therefore, abortion at any stage is murder and should be prevented. Pro-choice advocates believe that life begins either at birth or somewhat earlier along the nine-month continuum that is a normal pregnancy. They do not believe that life begins at conception. Aborting a pregnancy is not murder and may be permissible under certain circumstances at any stage.

If one believes that a fetus is a person at conception, then it follows that abortion at any stage means the taking of a human life, which is murder and, by definition, immoral. If, however, the fetus is not human until it reaches a certain stage of development, then abortion before that time does not constitute taking a human life.

The question of when life begins has been argued many times over. Professor Paul Campos at the University of Colorado explains it in this way: "Whether or not abortion should be legal turns on the question of whether and at what point a fetus is a person. The concept of personhood is . . . essentially a religious, or quasi religious idea, based on one's fundamental (and therefore unverifiable) assumptions about the nature of the world."

W. Kenneth Cauthen, professor emeritus of theology at Colgate Crozer Divinity School, writes: "The easy division of people into pro-life and pro-choice camps shows how complex issues are reduced to simple labels and slogans. The emergence of new life is a continuous process that proceeds over a period of nine months. Designating a specific point at which a potential person becomes an actual person is impossible."

Impossible or not, those on both sides of the question do try to answer it. The late President Ronald Reagan wrote while in office: "The real question today is not when human life begins, but, 'What is the value of human life?' . . . . The real question . . . is whether that tiny human life had a God-given right to be protected by law—the same right we all have."

But that is not the question for Janet Hadley in *Abortion: Between Freedom and Necessity*. She writes: "The question of 'rights' comes up all the time in the morality of abortion. If the fetus has a 'right to life,' this affects a woman's sexual and reproductive rights. It might even mean she must incubate an embryo and bear a child against her will. But can a woman's decision 'outrank' the rights of the fetus?"

If the issue is when life begins and if no one can prove it either way, can there ever be some kind of coming together? Perhaps it is best to consider the arguments on both sides before making a personal decision.

Pro-life advocates contend that abortion is murder for the following reasons: They claim that the fetus is a living human being, a one-of-a-kind person at the moment of conception. Even if you are an identical twin, there will never be another you in the entire history of the world. If the tiny, fertilized egg is a brand-new life, abortion, which will destroy it, is murder and, therefore, wrong. Abortion, says pro-life, is the murder of a unique child.

Furthermore, its advocates say that pro-life has been a concept throughout the history of the world. For instance, they point to the Bible, in which, in their interpretation, the unborn is often referred to as a child.

Although the issue is argued from many points, the end result for pro-life is the same: a human being begins at the moment of conception. Therefore, abortion, which takes away that human life, is murder—and, therefore, immoral.

The pro-choice view is very different. Abortion is not murder, advocates say; a fertilized egg is not a baby, just as a turtle egg is not a turtle and an acorn is not a tree. All have the potential, but they are not there yet. Advocates point out that nature itself is the biggest killer of fetuses; about 20 percent of pregnancies are naturally aborted, as are a certain number of fertilized eggs.

As for the argument that history and tradition support pro-life, that is untrue, claim pro-choice members. Abortion is never directly referred to in the Bible, nor is it forbidden. Ancient societies may have disapproved at various times, but, say pro-choice advocates, abortion was not seen as murder.

Abortion, according to most pro-choice people, is a difficult step that should never be taken lightly. But they believe that it is not a religious issue. They say that religious views should not dominate state policy. They believe that the fetus is not a child; abortion is not murder.

How Far Apart?

Pro-choice defenders want at least to keep the laws as they are. Pro-life defenders want to change the status quo. But both sides run the gamut of political opinions. Some pro-choice people think all abortions should be legal. Some think they should be legal but not into the third trimester. Some who are pro-life think that all abortions should be illegal. But some say that rape, incest, and certain medical conditions should be grounds for abortion. Therefore, fetal status is not always the key concern in the abortion issue.

Since the landmark decision in 1973, "pro-choice" and "pro-life" have become well-known terms. These labels have always been politically charged. Each side wants to be seen in the more favorable light, and each accuses the other of using loaded words. For instance, those against *Roe* v. *Wade* refer to themselves as pro-life, never as antiabortion. The term pro-life suggests that pro-choice people are anti-life, an assumption strongly challenged by those who agree with *Roe* v. *Wade*.

A pro-choice person speaks of the "fetus" or "embryo." The pro-life defenders might use "unborn child" or "pre-born infant." Each side also has a number of organizations that back their causes. Planned Parenthood Federation of America, NARAL Pro-Choice America, and Feminists Women's Health Center are leading pro-choice groups, as are most feminist organizations. Backers of pro-life include the National Right to Life Committee, the American Life League, and the American Association of Pro-Life Obstetricians and Gynecologists. In addition, there are a number of radical groups such as the pro-life Operation Rescue. Pro-choice groups have not been violent, but many on the other side, most especially the radical groups, have been involved in many instances of violence against abortion clinics–even murder. Some religious and conservative groups are antiabortion to some degree.

The country's major political parties also use the abortion issue to lure voters to their side. The Democratic platform generally supports *Roe* v. *Wade* and opposes most limits on it. In 2000 and 2004, the national platform supported safe abortions as well as those that are legal and rare. Legal refers to keeping government interference out of individual matters. Rare refers to the aim of using reproduction and contraceptive data to reduce the number of abortions. The Republican Party generally opposes *Roe* v. *Wade*. During its convention of 2004, Republicans restated the party's belief concerning the fundamental rights of the unborn child as well as its commitment to a human life amendment to the Constitution.

Both sides of the abortion issue are fervently devoted to their causes. They are so devoted to and so involved in the issue that little calm, rational debate occurs face-to-face. The two sides speak at great length on their differences, but rarely to each other. They make speeches and write books. But direct debate between the two sides is more likely to end in a shouting match than a calm appraisal of what separates them, or even perhaps what joins them.

Should Abortion Be a Woman's Personal Choice?

People on either side of the abortion controversy differ on when life begins. They also differ on a woman's personal choice and on the question of legality.

If one person believes abortion is murder and the other does not, obviously the two disagree about protecting a woman's personal choice. For pro-life advocates, the fetus has a right to life. That right must be upheld, which means that the woman's personal choice must be secondary. Abortion does not protect a woman's civil rights, they argue; in fact, it leads to a disregard for human life and fosters an atmosphere of violence and the shedding of responsibility.

Far from solving a woman's problems, say pro-life defenders, abortion may even make life more difficult. They point to various scientific studies that relate abortion to long-term mental and physical problems. They also feel that the heterosexual relationship that resulted in the pregnancy often will not survive the abortion experience. Women may come to regard their bodies with displeasure and physical intimacy with fear. In addition, if abortions are against the law, many women will think again before attempting an illegal procedure. Thus, say pro-life advocates, the number of abortions will be reduced.

They also state that abortions do not reduce the number of child abuse cases in the United States. Nor do abortions get rid of poor parents, bad parents, or single parents.

Although some pro-life advocates would permit abor-

ACTORS WHOOPI GOLDBERG AND CHRISTINE LAHTI (L) YELL AT
ANTIABORTION DEMONSTRATORS IN WASHINGTON, APRIL 25,
2004, DURING AN ABORTION RIGHTS RALLY AND MARCH. THE
DEBATE OVER ABORTION RIGHTS CONTINUES, WITH NO LESSENING
OF VEHEMENCE ON EITHER SIDE.

tions in the case of birth defects or rape or incest, many
would not. They argue that all life is valuable. They believe that aborting a fetus because of a potential birth de-
fect is aborting a person who has a right to life.

People who are pro-choice disagree with all those arguments. Abortion must remain a woman's decision, its
advocates say, if for no other reason than that she carries
the fetus within her body. In a free society, that must be the
law. A woman must not be held prisoner by a government

that requires her to bring an unwanted pregnancy to term. Since the abortion decision profoundly affects her own body, she alone must have the right to make such a choice.

Pro-choice advocates also question the idea that government or local organizations will train mothers to care for their children. They say that the very people who insist that all abortions be illegal are the same ones who want cutbacks in programs or services for poor or unmarried women. Abortions allow women personal freedom to compete in society. That right must be protected if men and women are to have an equal chance at success and personal happiness. By a vast majority, say pro-choice backers, women do not have abortions on a whim, or choose one thoughtlessly. Most abortions are performed for serious reasons that profoundly affect women's lives; that right must be upheld. An example might be a married woman who has a sick child to care for and her birth control fails. Her husband's job does not provide health insurance. She may have to make the difficult decision to have an abortion because the family cannot afford to raise another child.

Are Abortions Painful for the Fetus?

There is no definitive answer as to when a fetus feels pain, and pro-choice and pro-life advocates disagree. Some scientists say that a fetus cannot feel pain until at least week twenty-eight of the pregnancy because the nerve pathways have not yet been formed. The thalamus, that part of the brain that sends data to other areas of the body, doesn't form until about then. Without the thalamus, pain information cannot be processed. However, scientists on both sides of the abortion debate differ as to when the fetus feels pain.

Should Abortion Remain Legal?

Ever since *Roe* v. *Wade* became law, its defenders have been wary of any encroachments on the rights of women. Their opponents, mainly through changes in state laws, have been trying to bring the matter once again before the Supreme Court, hoping to change the decision.

As a practical matter, pro-choice advocates do not believe that outlawing abortions once again will eliminate them. They say that those women who can afford them will go to countries where abortions are legal. Those who cannot will simply go underground, where not only fetuses but many women will die.

Pro-life advocates claim that many women choose the abortion option just because it is so available. If it were illegal, they believe many would decide against the procedure simply to avoid going to jail or paying a heavy fine. Even if a certain number of women still chose abortions, at least some of the unborn would be saved if the procedure were illegal.

Many pro-life backers believe that abortions should be illegal even in the case of rape or incest. They argue that the child is not responsible for the circumstances of its conception and should not pay the price with death. They cite improving medical advances as one reason to allow a child with birth defects to be born. And they question who has the right to decide what constitutes an acceptable quality of life.

Stem Cell Research

Another argument between pro-choice and pro-life advocates concerns stem cell research. Although the controversy is fairly new, the research itself is not. In the 1800s, scientists learned that some cells could generate other cells.

These so-called stem cells have the ability to grow into nearly any kind of cell. That opens endless doors for medical advancement. For instance, damaged neural cords in the spine may be replaced with stem cells. That offers the hope that paralyzed people will walk again. Cells in the brain or heart or liver—or elsewhere in the body—that have been destroyed by cancer treatments may be replaced by new, healthy stem cells and the organ will function again.

Scientists warn that such promising cures are at best a decade away. Doctors admit that the science is still in the early stages. But to many, the possibilities seem endless. Why is there disagreement today over this area of research? Who would be against the possibility of such outstanding medical advances? In truth, the major fight is not over research or medical cures. The trouble centers on the source of cells that are available for the research.

There are two types of stem cells: embryonic and adult. Embryonic stem cells (ESC) come from embryos developed from eggs that have been fertilized outside the body (in vitro, meaning in the lab, fertilization, or IVF). The cells are taken from a microscopic ball of cells called the blastocyst. Embryonic stem cells have totipotency, which means they can develop into all cell types. A plant cutting, for example, can be used to produce an entire plant.

Adult stem cells are found in tissue that has differentiated beyond the blastocyst stage. So, whereas embryonic cells can form a human being, adult stem cells cannot. They have pluripotency, meaning they can form most but not all cell types. The main role of adult stem cells is to maintain and repair the tissue in which they are found.

Cord cells are extracted from the umbilical cord during pregnancy. The umbilical cord, which connects the fetus to the mother and is removed after birth, is a

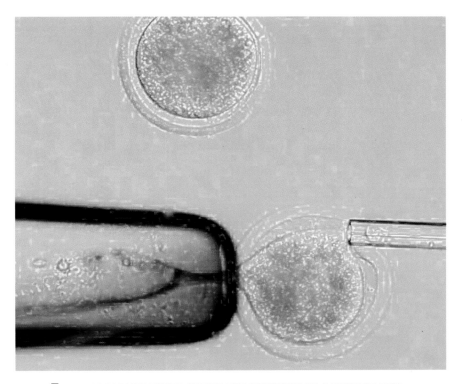

THIS MICROSCOPIC PHOTO SHOWS THE INJECTION OF A SOMATIC CELL INTO A NUCLEAR-REMOVED HUMAN EGG CELL DURING AN EXPERIMENT IN SOUTH KOREA. RESEARCHERS THERE CLAIMED THAT IT HAD CLONED A HUMAN EMBRYO AND EXTRACTED EMBRYONIC STEM CELLS FROM THE CLONE. THE EXISTENCE OF THIS CLONE, HOWEVER, HAS NEVER BEEN PROVEN.

rich source of stem cells. They are stored in cell banks to be used later for the newborn or the mother, father, or others. The closer the relationship between donor and donee, the better the chance that the cells will not be rejected. The storing of these cells is much like blood bank storage.

Extracted stem cells from the embryo can be kept alive indefinitely. Grown in cultures, they double in number about every two to three days. A set of cells from one blastocyst is called a stem cell line. James Thompson of the University of Wisconsin in Madison was the first to develop an embryonic stem cell line in 1998.

Typically, the blastocysts used in this kind of research come from in vitro fertilization procedures. Any number of medical problems can cause infertility. For infertile couples, IVF unites their egg and sperm in vitro. After the union, the fertilized egg is transferred to the uterus, and pregnancy begins when the egg is implanted in the uterine lining.

When stem cells are taken from this type of blastocyst, the blastocyst is destroyed. Pro-life advocates claim this is murder, and they want all such procedures involving embryonic cells to be stopped. Pro-choice backers say the tiny blastocyst does not have any human features. Some people are against embryonic stem cell research on medical grounds.

There is some evidence that these cells tend to become cancerous when injected into humans. Embryonic cells do not respond to the differentiation signals that the other cells send. This does not happen with adult stem cells.

Stem cell research in the United States was originally halted by President George W. Bush, but in 2001, because of political pressure, it was allowed to resume in government labs. Researchers working on already-existing embryonic stem cell lines received federal money, but no new lines could be developed. As of fall 2006, only twenty-one viable lines remained, and they are old lines. Scientists say it wastes money and time to work with them.

In May 2005, the House of Representatives tried to ease the problem by passing a bill that allowed government-funded research on surplus embryos in fertility clinics. Bush vetoed the bill in July 2006. Some scientists argue that the government's failure to fund this research puts the United States further and further behind in such technol-

Pros and Cons of Embryonic Stem Cell Research

According to an article in *Time* magazine, these are the arguments on both sides:

"Opponents of ESC research—starting with [President Geroge W.] Bush—argue that you can't destroy life in order to save it; supporters argue that an eight-cell embryo doesn't count as a human life in the first place—not when compared with the life it could help save. Opponents say embryo research has been oversold. . . . Supporters retort that adult stem cells are still of limited use . . . we can learn only from studying leftover fertility-clinic embryos that would otherwise be thrown away.

"Back and forth it goes, the politics driving the science, the science pushing back."

Time, August 7, 2006, pp. 41–42.

ogy. Countries such as Great Britain and Japan are pioneers in this field.

Embryonic stem cell research is not banned in state-funded or private labs in the United States. In 2002, California passed the first law in the country to allow it. In June 2006, Harvard University announced a multimillion-dollar, privately funded project to create cloned human embryos to generate stem cells. The procedure will fuse a person's body cells, such as a skin cell, with a human egg from which the DNA is removed. The result is a cell identical to the donor. The hoped-for results will be used in the treatment of diabetes, leukemia, sickle-cell anemia, and Lou Gehrig's disease.

With the announcement, then Harvard president Lawrence Summers acknowledged the controversy in this field. He said, "While we understand and respect the sincerely held beliefs of those who oppose the research, we are equally sincere in our belief that the life-and-death medical needs of countless suffering children and adults justifies moving forward with this research."

Rights of Minors and Other Special Cases

With few restrictions, adult women in the United States have the right to choose abortion as an option. But what are the options for a pregnant teenager? And what are the rights of pregnant women serving terms in prison? Should fathers have a say in abortions? The choice of abortion is always a serious decision and certain circumstances can make the decision even more complicated.

The Rights of Minors

A minor generally has the right to an abortion in the United States with one major restriction: parents must agree to the procedure or at least be told about it. Thirty-five of the fifty states currently have laws that say one or both parents must be notified or must give consent. Nine states have parental laws not yet in effect. Six states, plus Washington, D.C., do not require a parent's involvement. A 2003 report in *American Psychologist* indicated that when minors become pregnant, "many, if not most, adolescents voluntarily tell their parents. Studies have reported widely varying numbers ranging from 35% to 91% of adolescents who inform their parents even when parental consent is not mandated; younger adolescents are more likely to inform their parents than are older adolescents."

Just as they differ over abortion for adults, pro-life and pro-choice defenders differ over the abortion rights of minors. Should parents be involved when the abortion seeker is not of legal age? Yes, say most pro-life advocates; no, say most people who are pro-choice.

In general, most pro-life advocates believe that a parent's involvement in an abortion should be treated like any other matter in society. Parents are legally responsible for their minor children, they point out. A minor cannot enter the military or even go on a school trip without a parent's consent. A hospital will not treat a minor, except in a life-saving situation, without getting parental approval. Why should abortion be different?

Pro-life advocates feel that parental involvement will reduce the number of abortions. They say that minors who are able to talk to their parents will be less likely to choose abortion. They feel that if parents are involved, the minor will be healthier because a young woman who is hiding her pregnancy is less likely to take care of herself physically. They also point to a likelihood of depression and other severe psychological problems for the minor who is hiding her pregnancy.

However, pro-life defenders acknowledge that every minor does not live in an intact nuclear family. A parent may be a drug addict, may be abusive, may have severe mental or physical problems, or may even be the one who committed incest. In such cases, laws in some states allow grandparents to make a decision. Other states involve the courts as the potential decisionmaker. Massachusetts, for instance, gives the minor the option of obtaining parental or judicial consent before an abortion.

Involving the parents, say pro-life people, alerts them to both physical and mental problems in their children. This in turn promotes stronger family bonds. Teenagers need guidance in making an informed choice over the serious matter of abortion. Parental involvement will strengthen the family, not destroy it.

The pro-choice side disagrees with these arguments. Abortion should be treated differently when it comes to parental involvement, they say, because it *is* different. Most states allow minors to get treatment for venereal disease without getting their parents' approval. They can even receive prenatal care without the consent of parents. Pro-choice advocates say that is because it is recognized that parental consent laws generally deter a minor from, rather than aid her in, obtaining medical help when pregnancy or abortion is involved. In fact, studies point out that about one-quarter of all minors would not tell parents of a pregnancy no matter what the law. The major reason is the expected abuse that will follow, either physical or verbal. In some cases, minors may not tell parents because they are traumatized by the thought of hurting them.

In any case, it is not clear that parental involvement reduces the number of abortions. Massachusetts passed a parental consent law in 1981 requiring minors to get a parent's consent before an abortion. A study reported in the *American Journal of Public Health* in 1986 said that minors continued to become pregnant, to give birth, and to have abortions in just about the same proportions both before and after the law. In March 2006, the *New England Journal of Medicine* published a study that followed the effects of a parental consent law in Texas since 2000. It concluded that the law was effective because the abortion decline for minors was greater than the abortion decline for non-minors. The decline was greatest among the youngest girls.

Teens with Autism and Developmental Disabilities

A *Newsday* article of July 18, 2006, reports that teens with autism or other developmental disabilities have a greater than average chance of being sexually molested by age eighteen. More than fifteen thousand are raped each year. Too often, notes the article, these teens are not given birth control or information about HIV because people don't think they have sexual needs like the average teenager. Most teenagers can spot dangerous situations and soon learn how to get out of them. But those who are autistic or have other developmental problems may be too naïve about such matters to keep themselves out of trouble. The article warns that parents and other adults in authority should be prepared to keep these minors as well informed as other teenagers.

Preventing Adolescent Pregnancy

Advocates on either side of the abortion issue would like to see a drop in adolescent pregnancies. Many medical experts believe the way to achieve that goal is through family-planning services.

In the 1990s, a survey was taken of family-planning services in the United States compared with those in Britain, the Netherlands, and Sweden. U.S. adolescent birth rates are among the highest in the industrialized world. They have declined, however, in recent years to

TEENS WHO HAVE CHOSEN TO HAVE CHILDREN OFTEN NEED MORE HELP THAN THEY CAN GET AT HOME. HERE, PREGNANT YOUNG WOMEN HOLD DOLLS AS THEY ATTEND A COUNSELING PROGRAM ON HOW TO CARE FOR THEIR CHILDREN.

about 64 per 1,000 teens between ages fifteen and nineteen. That compares with 33 per 1,000 in Britain, 7 in the Netherlands, and 5 in Sweden.

In Sweden, there is a large network of youth clinics staffed mainly by nurse-midwives. The care is free, as it is in maternity clinics. In the Netherlands, contraceptive devices are provided mainly by doctors at no fee. Clinics offer family-planning services. Britain offers contraception services paid by the National Health Service. In the United States, teenagers receive family-planning services at facilities such as Planned Parenthood and some local health departments. They are also available in some private offices and clinics. The cost of family-planning services is paid for by public insurance; many private insurance companies do not cover it. Teenagers in the United States generally face more barriers in gaining access to contraceptive services than do minors in Europe.

Pregnant Behind Bars

Today, there are about 104,000 women in U.S. prisons, out of a total inmate population of about 1,400,000. Although far fewer in number, the female prison population is growing faster than the number of male inmates, mostly because of drug charges. A Justice Department report estimates that about 5 percent of female prisoners are pregnant when they are jailed. The Sentencing Project, a nonprofit organization in Washington, D.C., says that about 40,000 women enter U.S. jails each year. Using that figure, about 2,000 babies are born in U.S. prisons annually. The high rates of sexual assault in prison and the generally low levels of health care often lead to pregnancy. In addition, throughout the prison system there is wide variation in a woman's access of health care and in the ability to exercise one's rights.

The U.S. prison system was essentially designed for males. Laws differ widely from state to state regarding female inmates in general and especially those who are pregnant. Both the federal Bureau of Prisons and eleven states have residential programs for inmate mothers. In federal prison, infants are allowed to stay with their mothers for only three months after delivery. The time differs in state institutions. Some states also offer parent education programs. In both California and Texas, female inmates have access to more parent education programs than do male inmates. In states without residential programs, the children are removed from their mothers either during the hospital stay or immediately afterward.

In a number of states it is still standard practice for a prisoner in labor to be shackled or chained to her bed during delivery. The usual method is to chain one wrist and one ankle. Only California and Illinois legally forbid this treatment. Illinois was the first state to do so, passing a law in 2000. New York is presently considering a ban on similar restraints. Said assemblywoman Sally J. Lieber of Mountain View, California, after California's non-restraint law was passed, "We found this was going on in some institutions in California and all over the United States. It presents risks not only for the inmate giving birth, but also for the infant."

In its defense, Dina Tyler of the Arkansas Department of Corrections said, "They [pregnant women] are still convicted felons, and sometimes violent in nature."

Practices also vary widely from state to state for women who seek abortions while in prison. In New Jersey, for instance, a pregnant prisoner can have an abortion up to eighteen weeks into the pregnancy. The state makes all the arrangements for the procedure, even escorting the woman to Planned Parenthood for counseling. Pennsylvania, along with thirteen other states, has no official written policy on abortion for prison inmates. North Carolina has no written policy, but it does have what is called established practice, meaning that it follows what it has become customary to do. Prenatal care and delivery at a hospital are paid for. Women in jail in Delaware must pay for their abortions, including a one-hundred-dollar charge for transportation to the clinic. Nine states—California, Connecticut, Georgia, Hawaii, New Jersey, New York, Oregon, Vermont, and Washington—allow access to abortion as well as counseling. All except Georgia fund abortions through Medicaid programs.

Massachusetts, Minnesota, Nevada, New Mexico, Tennessee, and the District of Columbia—fund abortions if they are medically necessary or therapeutic. But since most of the states rarely define those terms, the result is often confusion. Minnesota, however, does explain the terms: Medicaid will pay for an inmate's therapeutic abortion in Minnesota if the woman has a life-threatening condition caused by the pregnancy; the pregnancy is the result of rape or incest; or the abortion is necessary for other health reasons.

Missouri is one state where the law prohibits the spending of public funds "for the purpose of performing or assisting an abortion not necessary to save the life of the mother." In 2005, Missouri prison officials refused to transport a woman prisoner to a clinic for an abortion. A federal judge overruled and ordered the woman to be taken to the clinic.

Abortions in Late Term

Late-term abortion is called partial birth abortion by the popular press, but dilation and extraction, or D & X, by the doctors who developed the procedure. This procedure involves collapsing the skull of the fetus and bringing it otherwise intact through the birth canal. Reasons given for its use include a severely malformed fetus or the endangerment of the woman's life if the pregnancy continues. Ever since the procedure was first described in 1993, it has set off fierce debate.

Congress passed the Partial Birth Abortion Ban Act in 1997, but it was vetoed by President Bill Clinton. He said the ban did not allow for a D & X to be performed to protect a woman's health. Passed again in 2003, it was signed into law by President George W. Bush. However, it was immediately challenged by federal judges in California, Nebraska, and New York. The law has never been enforced. However, in late 2006 the Supreme Court agreed to hear an appeal concerning the Nebraska ban in the case of *Gonzales v. Carhart*. Once again, at the center of the issue was whether the ban endangers the health of women under certain circumstances. The bill passed by Congress does not specifically provide a general exemption for a woman's health. However, it does state that the ban "does not apply to a partial-birth abortion that is necessary to save the life of a mother whose life is endangered by a physical disorder, physical illness, or physical injury, including a life-endangering physical condition caused by or arising from the pregnancy itself."

Legislation passed in Missouri in 1999 indicates how the states have used the law to try to infringe on the Supreme Court ruling. Called the Infant's Protection Act and passed by right-to-life legislators over the governor's veto, the law calls infanticide any act that causes the death of a fetus outside or partly outside the womb. Infanticide is a felony.

The law makes illegal what is referred to as partial birth abortion, which some thirty other states have done. But the Missouri law went further. Critics claim that the language of the law reaches back to pertain to the fifth and

Partial Birth Abortion Laws

In recent years, the Supreme Court has struck down four laws concerning partial birth abortion because the laws did not provide exceptions that protected a woman's health:

June 1, 2004. *Planned Parenthood Federation of America* v. *Ashcroft.* District court of San Francisco overturns a state law.

August 26, 2004. *National Abortion Federation* v. *Ashcroft.* Federal District Court of New York nullifies a federal law.

June 3, 2005. *Richmond Medical Center* v. *Hicks.* Decision of a lower court in Virginia to strike down a state law is upheld in the U.S. Court of Appeals for the Fourth Circuit.

July 8, 2005. *Carhart* v. *Gonzales.* Eighth District Court of Appeals upholds decision of lower court to nullify a federal law.

sixth weeks of pregnancy. Under this ruling, those who perform this procedure are subject to life in prison.

Fathers and Sperm Donors

Do husbands and/or fathers have a legal say in the abortion issue? In its *Roe v. Wade* ruling, the Supreme Court left that question to the woman and her doctor to decide. Once again, there is argument over the issue. The majority of those who favor *Roe v. Wade* maintain that since the woman must physically bear the child, including the complications that might result, her decision must be the final one. Paternal rights advocates claim it is unfair to give a woman greater reproductive liberty. She can choose to bear the child, place it for adoption, or have an abortion. This leaves the father with emotional and even financial consequences, even though he is not consulted in the decision. Advocates say the biological father should have the right to give consent or at least be told if an abortion is planned.

Historically, paternal rights have often been protected. There are several cases in Roman law where the woman was either exiled or sentenced to death for having an abortion. The law said she had denied her husband the rights of a father. In most countries today the issue remains unclear. In Egypt, Iraq, Morocco, and Turkey, for instance, the law says that a woman must have her husband's consent before having an abortion. However, that law is usually ignored if the woman's health is in question. In the United States, a number of states have paternal notification laws that have yet to be tested.

When There Is No Option

Roe v. Wade did not tell women to have abortions; it provided them with the *option* of choosing whether to have a child. Throughout history, that option has often been denied, not only by banning abortions but by what is called compulsory sterilization.

The most infamous programs of compulsory sterilization were those of Nazi Germany before and during World War II. Some four hundred thousand people, male and female, were sterilized in the 1930s and 1940s. The purpose was mainly to get rid of what the Nazis called unfit people, meaning those from certain ethnic groups or those who were mentally or physically disabled in some way.

Eugenics is concerned with controlling the hereditary qualities of a race of people. Beginning in about 1900 and continuing through the 1970s, some sixty-five thousand people were sterilized in the United States. Most of the victims were mentally retarded or mentally ill. However, a number of state laws also targeted those who were blind, deaf, or physically disabled. In addition, there are reports of Native Americans who were sterilized, as were some prison inmates. At least some of the sterilizations took place without the person's knowledge, for example, while a woman was in the hospital giving birth.

In 1907, Indiana became the first state to legalize sterilization. At first, not many states followed. However, in 1927, the Supreme Court, in *Buck v. Bell*, decided that a home for the mentally retarded in Virginia had the right to sterilize its patients.

The case involved an eighteen-year-old rape victim, Carrie Buck, who was living in the home, as was her mother. A test of the young woman's I.Q. revealed a mental age of nine. The prosecutor presented her as being not only feebleminded, but morally delinquent. The Court agreed that she should be sterilized. After that, the number of sterilizations in the United States increased until 1942 and another Supreme Court decision. In *Skinner v. Oklahoma*, a man who was twice convicted for armed robbery

SARAH JANE WILEY STARES OUT THE WINDOW OF A FORMER
OPERATING ROOM FOR THE EPILEPTIC AND FEEBLEMINDED IN
LYNCHBURG, VIRGINIA. WILEY WAS ONE OF THOUSANDS OF PEOPLE—
MOSTLY TEENAGERS—STERILIZED IN THE NAME OF EUGENICS IN
THIS OPERATING ROOM OVER THE COURSE OF FIFTY YEARS BEFORE
THE PRACTICE WAS OUTLAWED. WILEY AND HER BROTHER WERE
STERILIZED IN 1959.

was ordered to be sterilized under the Oklahoma Criminal Sterilization Act. In June 1942, the Court ruled against Oklahoma 9 to 0. It said there was no reason to conclude that the tendency to commit robbery was an inherited trait.

With the country at that time involved in World War II and with stories of German atrocities beginning to surface, America's view of sterilization began to change. However, the procedures continued in some states through the 1960s. Oregon was the last state to allow an enforced sterilization, in 1981. A number of states, including Virginia, Oregon, and California, which sterilized more people than any other, have apologized for their programs in recent years.

4

Rape and Incest

Sometimes the victims of rape or incest become pregnant from that criminal act. How are they protected by law? Do they have the option of abortion in all cases?

Rape is a serious and violent crime. Generally, it refers to sexual intercourse by a man against a woman without her consent, through force or the threat of force. However, rape can also be committed against another man and by a woman against a man. Statutory rape means a sexual act against a child or an adult who is not able to understand the meaning of sexual intercourse.

Contrary to oft-told tales, the rapist is not always a stranger hiding in a dark alley with a gun or in a deserted parking garage at midnight. Four out of ten assaults take place in the victim's own home; nearly two-thirds of all rapes are committed by someone the person knows; more than half occur within a mile of where the individual lives. According to the Rape, Abuse & Incest National Network, nine out of every ten rape victims are female. Eighty percent of all victims are white. Eighty percent of victims

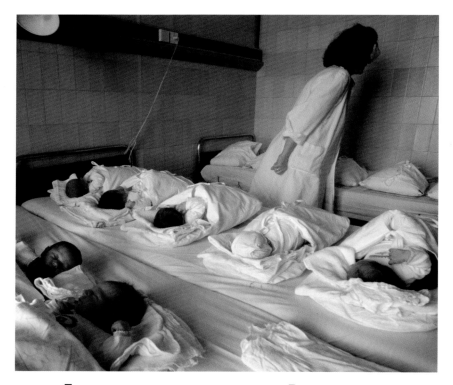

THIS MATERNITY HOSPITAL IS PACKED WITH BOSNIAN REFUGEES WHO WERE RAPED IN THE COURSE OF THE CONFLICT WITH SERBIA. THESE BABIES WERE TO BE TURNED OVER TO A CATHOLIC HUMANITARIAN ORGANIZATION FOR ADOPTION BY WOMEN IN OTHER LANDS WHO WOULD NOT ASSOCIATE THESE BABIES WITH THEIR TRAUMA.

are less than thirty years old, and 29 percent are aged twelve to seventeen. In instances of assaults against juveniles, 93 percent know their attackers.

Yet, for all the numbers and all the violence, rape is one of the least-reported crimes in the United States. More than 60 percent of rapes and sexual assaults are not reported to police. And those who do report the crime rarely do so immediately.

Why is rape so underreported? The reasons are many, but often they have to do with sexist attitudes toward women. For some people, there is always the suspicion that the woman is somehow at fault. For many women, the personal stigma of rape is a barrier. The rape victim is also less likely to report the crime without support from family, health centers, and law enforcement agencies. Law enforcement itself has a long history of paying little attention to rape crimes and victims. Pressure from women's organizations and other groups, and from women themselves, has resulted in more serious treatment of rape victims by police agencies.

The U.S. criminal justice system does have the power to help victims. It has the authority to arrest, convict, and punish rapists. The National Crime Victimization Survey says that, following a rape report to police, there is a 50 percent chance of an arrest.

Arrest does not always result in conviction, however. In some cases, the victim is unable to identify the assailant. The states have various laws covering the proof required before a suspect is arrested or prosecuted. In addition, in many states there is a statute of limitations on rape, meaning that, unlike murder, a suspect cannot be prosecuted after a certain number of years.

Effects of Rape

Rape usually results in physical harm and psychological trauma. Victims deal with trauma in different ways. However, victims of sexual assaults are very likely to suffer from depression and posttraumatic stress disorder. They may abuse alcohol and drugs. Some attempt suicide, and some succeed. It is important for a rape victim to receive medical and psychological assistance as soon as possible.

Posttraumatic Stress Disorder in Rape Victims

A common result of experiencing a sexual assault is called Rape-Related Posttraumatic Stress Disorder. It has four major symptoms:

Re-experiencing the trauma: Rape victims may experience recurrent nightmares or flashbacks about the rape, or may have an inability to stop remembering the rape.

Social withdrawal: This symptom involves the inability to experience feelings of any kind.

Avoidance behaviors and actions: Victims may desire to avoid any feelings and thoughts that might recall to mind events about the rape.

Increased physiological arousal characteristics: This symptom can be marked by an exaggerated startle response, hypervigilance, sleep disorders, or difficulty concentrating. *

*Rape, Abuse & Incest National Network

Treatment and the Law

In addition to trauma, rape victims may have the fear of a pregnancy resulting from the crime. According to the National Crime Victimization Survey, about 5 percent of rapes result in a pregnancy. There were more than 65,000 victims of rape in 2004. Using that figure, about 3,000 cases resulted in a pregnancy for that year.

A woman reporting a rape is generally taken to a hospital emergency room or similar facility immediately. There she may be given emergency contraception, or EC (also known as the morning-after pill). As described in the November 2005 fact sheet of the Henry J. Kaiser Family Foundation: "Emergency contraception is a pre-packaged dose of pills containing the hormone progestin, the same hormone found in daily oral contraceptives. . . . EC does not affect an established pregnancy."

As with many laws dealing with pregnancy and abortion, there is much confusion in the states concerning the use of EC. Although EC is endorsed by major medical associations such as the American College of Obstetricians and Gynecologists (ACOG) and the American Medical Association, the laws differ widely. Many hospitals do not offer it. As noted on the Planned Parenthood Web site: "There is mounting evidence that some hospitals, especially religion-based hospitals, are not providing EC to sexual assault survivors."

In 2005, two bills were introduced in Congress—HR2928 and S1264—requiring all hospitals receiving federal funds to offer EC to women in cases of assault.

Eight states—California, Massachusetts, New Jersey, New York, Ohio, Oregon, South Carolina, and Virginia—now direct the ER staff to offer EC in rape cases. Only four states—California, Massachusetts, New Mexico, and Washington—require the emergency room to offer EC. In

REDMOND HIGH SCHOOL LIBRARY

most states, a woman must get a doctor's prescription for EC. Arkansas, California, Hawaii, Massachusetts, Maine, New Hampshire, New Mexico, and Washington allow her to get it directly from a pharmacist.

Pro-choice and pro-life groups disagree on whether EC is birth control or an abortifacient (meaning an agent that induces abortion). According to the Religious Tolerance Web site: "There is general agreement among pro-choice groups, and medical professionals, that emergency contraception is a contraceptive. It does not induce abortions. In the event that a pregnancy has begun, that is, a blastocyst has been implanted in the wall of the uterus—the medication has no effect. Pro-life groups . . . maintain that these pills can and sometimes do induce an abortion."

EC: Sometimes Difficult to Get

Although it is legal to administer emergency contraception and to dispense information about it, women may have difficulty in obtaining this help at various medical facilities. The Catholic Church has often been singled out as refusing to provide EC. A 2005 article by Molly Ginty of *Women's e News* reports: "Even though many state laws require hospitals to offer emergency contraception after sexual assault, rape survivors who go to Catholic hospitals may find that it is not, in fact, offered to them." However, the St. Louis-based Catholic Health Association of the United States says that "most Catholic hospitals test for a pregnancy that occurred before and is unrelated to the sexual assault. If the pregnancy test is negative, the woman is offered emergency contraception."

The Catholic Church operates the nation's largest single group of nonprofit medical facilities in the United States. Its hospitals make up about 12 percent of the nearly five thousand community hospitals in the United

States. A community hospital, according to the American Hospital Association (AHA), covers nonfederal, short-term general, and other special hospitals, such as rehabilitation or orthopedic institutions. The total number of yearly admissions to these facilities is more than thirty-five million. In addition, about 15 percent of all emergency room visits in the United States are to Catholic hospitals.

Catholic hospitals in the United States operate under these rules: abortion is not permitted even in cases of rape or incest; emergency contraception is not provided to victims of sexual assault; the hospital staff cannot offer transportation to another institution where abortions are performed. Often these restrictions most significantly affect poor women seeking abortions, or women seeking abortions or any kind of birth control services in rural areas. Catholic hospitals may be the only medical facilities in a rural area because they often operate as charitable institutions. In urban areas, women are more likely to have a choice of hospitals where abortion services are offered.

Even in non-Catholic hospitals, a victim cannot always get emergency treatment quickly. Some hospitals have the drug on-site, but more don't. Some give the victim a prescription, and she must find a pharmacist to fill it. Some demand that the woman get the prescription herself from an independent doctor and then have a pharmacist fill it. By that time the drug may be useless because it is no longer the morning after.

In August 2006, the U.S. Food and Drug Administration (FDA) approved the sale of Plan B, the morning-after pill, without a prescription (so-called over-the-counter) to women age eighteen and older. After a three-year battle within the FDA, the decision was considered a compromise by pro-choice advocates. They had hoped that the pill would have been approved for women regardless of age. If taken within seventy-two hours after unprotected sex, Plan B is judged to be 89 percent effective in preventing pregnancy.

Those who support Plan B believe that the number of unwanted pregnancies in the United States each year will be cut in half because of its over-the-counter availability. But many pro-life advocates disagree. They fear that such easy access to the pill might foster sexual promiscuity, which could lead to more unwanted pregnancies. But pro-choice advocates feel that the pill will not promote promiscuity and that it is just one more chance to stop an unintended pregnancy.

Since 1999, Plan B has been available in the United States with a prescription. Some pharmacists in a few states, such as California, were allowed to write prescriptions for the pill if they received special training. The over-the-counter pill will be sold only in pharmacies (that includes those in convenience and grocery stores). It must be kept in a locked cabinet or behind the counter.

EC and the Pharmacist

The change in abortion laws in the United States puts a spotlight on the importance of pharmacies and the pharmacist. In most areas, a woman who has been raped, for instance, is taken to a hospital or clinic for examination and administration of the so-called morning-after pill. It is also legal for pharmacies to stock these pills. However, since *Roe* v. *Wade*, there have been numerous instances of pharmacists refusing to dispense abortion and contraceptive medications because of religious beliefs.

For example, a pharmacist in Wisconsin refused to fill a prescription for oral contraceptives. He said it was against his religious principles. In 2005, he was reprimanded by the state pharmacy board, which set limits on his pharmacy license. A much publicized case involving

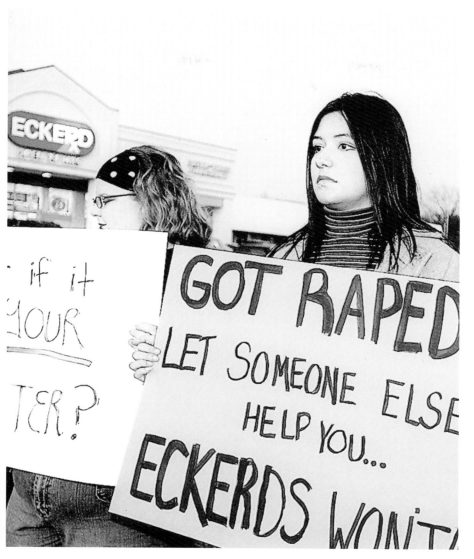

CONTROVERSY PERSISTS OVER WHETHER PHARMACISTS MUST LEGALLY
PRESCRIBE DRUGS OF WHICH THEY DISAPPROVE. ABOUT FORTY PEOPLE
GATHERED OUTSIDE AN ECKERD'S PHARMACY IN FEBRUARY 2004
PROTESTING WHAT THEY SAID WAS A DECISION TO DENY A RAPE
VICTIM A MORNING-AFTER PILL.

pharmacists occurred in Denton, Texas, in March 2004. Three pharmacists at a large chain drugstore refused to give emergency contraceptive pills to a rape victim. All three said they did so on religious grounds. They were fired.

In April 2005, Arizona governor Janet Napolitano vetoed a law that said pharmacists could refuse to sell birth control and morning-after pills. "Pharmacies and other health care service providers have no right to interfere in the lawful personal medical decisions made by patients and their doctors," she said. In a similar decision, Illinois governor Rod Blagojevich added an emergency amendment to the state code. It requires pharmacists to give out such medication even if it goes against their religious beliefs. The American Center for Law and Justice is challenging the governor's action.

In 2006, the Cedar River Clinics, an abortion provider in several cities in the state of Washington, filed a complaint with the state Department of Health. It cited three instances in which pharmacists refused to fill patients' prescriptions on the basis of moral objections. The state Board of Pharmacy in Washington is beginning debate on rules to determine if pharmacists have the right to use moral, religious, or other grounds to refuse prescriptions.

Once again, pro-life and pro-choice advocates differ. Sara Ainsworth of Northwest Women's Law Center (NWLC) says: "Federal and state laws are clear: Employers can require employees to meet a 'bona fide occupational qualification.' If you're a pharmacist, it's your job to dispense drugs if there are no problems like drug interactions." But the Alliance Defense Fund, a Christian group from Arizona, disagrees: "The right of conscience is a fundamental right recognized in the Washington Constitution. No citizen can be forced to yield that right when he or she enters the profession of his choice."

Does Rape Justify Abortion?

Few on either side of the abortion argument would deny that a sexual assault of any kind is an horrific experience for any victim. And it is true that only a small percentage of abortions are performed because of rape. However, if a rape does result in a pregnancy, does that justify abortion?

To pro-choice advocates and institutions, the question should not even be asked. Abortion is a legal option in the United States. In opposition, whereas many pro-life advocates acknowledge the trauma of the experience, they feel that destroying a human being is worse than giving birth to the child of a rapist. Do not punish the child for the way in which it was conceived, they say. Killing the unborn will not take away the sorrow of rape.

Some people who might ordinarily be considered pro-life on the question of abortion do feel that it is justified in the case of rape or incest. Many religious institutions agree. Among those that regard abortion as an acceptable option are the American Baptist Churches-USA, the American Friends (Quaker) Service Committee, the American Jewish Congress, the Episcopal Church (USA), and the United Methodist Church. Some religious institutions that recognize abortion as an option only when the pregnancy results from rape or incest include the Southern Baptist Church and the Church of Jesus Christ of Latter-day Saints (Mormons).

Incest or Birth Defects

Many pro-life advocates feel that there is never a reason for an abortion. But many who are otherwise antiabortion make an exception for pregnancies that result from incest or those that will end with the birth of a seriously deformed child. They agree with the argument that the resulting child is innocent of how it was conceived. Yet, they argue, it would be unthinkable to insist that a thirteen-year-old girl be forced to give birth to a child fathered by her own father.

On the question of abortion when the child would be seriously mentally and/or physically deformed, pro-life advocates say that any life is better than no life at all. But not everyone agrees. Some believe that a short life filled with pain and difficulty, sometimes with little or no awareness of senses, may not count as a life. It is only modern technology, they contend, that keeps alive many children with birth defects who would otherwise die within a short time. Not only are these children condemned to a life of suffering, but so are their parents.

Some women may choose to keep a child with birth defects even in very severe cases when the child has no chance of any mental or physical development. Some women may choose to bear a child from a sexual assault. That is their right, say pro-choice advocates. But it is also a woman's right to end such a pregnancy in abortion.

Who Pays?

When state Medicaid funding will not pay for abortions, whether resulting from rape or otherwise, low-income women can't always afford the procedure. There are a number of abortion funds operating throughout the United States in various states. The National Network of Abortion Funds (NNAF) gives support and technical aid to these local organizations. Member funds help about twenty-two thousand women a year, many of them victims of sexual assault. Even when federal law requires abortion funding in cases of rape, many state agencies still deny the operation.

The cost of an abortion in the United States varies

widely. Estimates put an abortion in the first trimester between $350 and $650. According to an article in *Commonwealth* in 1994, about 80 percent of private health insurance policies cover the costs of an abortion.

Abortion, Race, and Religion

In April 2004, a huge crowd gathered on the National Mall in Washington, D.C. More than a million women and men took part in the March for Women's Lives. They were protesting policies—both national and local—that threaten to overturn *Roe* v. *Wade*. For the first time, minority organizations such as the Black Women's Health Imperative (BWHI) and National Latina Institute for Reproductive Health joined the other marchers, which included Planned Parenthood and the National Organization for Women (NOW). The event reflected expanding leadership that was once predominantly all-white and a broader agenda, emphasized by the name of the event, formerly the March for Choice.

When Race Makes a Difference

Since the push to liberalize abortion laws began in the 1960s, black women, as well as other minorities, have rarely been a major part of it. This may seem surprising in view of past discrimination against minorities. However, according to Toni M. Bond, executive director for the National Network of Abortion Funds, "Black women have been and still are treated as 'invited guests' in the reproductive rights movement."

According to statistics, black women between the ages of eighteen and twenty-four who earn less than $15,000 a year have abortions at twice the rate of the general population. Lorraine Cole of the Black Women's Health Imperative cited a lack of family-planning information as well as a general lack of readily obtainable health care services as two of the reasons for the many unintended pregnancies. She also noted that black women have fewer options for abortion because so many are poor and there are now fewer health services for those on Medicaid.

Studies show that the experience of motherhood and family life is quite different for black and white women. Discrimination through the years brought higher rates of unemployment for black males, one of the factors that disrupt family life. That led to black women working longer and taking charge of families more often than white women. Studies also show a somewhat different attitude toward abortion between blacks and whites. In general, black women tend to be less positive about the procedure. That is in part because of a family history of religious beliefs. Also, black women tend to have less access to abortion support facilities. An article in *Feminist Issues* in the 1990s reflected: "It is not that black women are not pro-choice; rather, they are 'pro-sex, pro-woman, pro-choice.' Women of color, and working class women in the United States in general, object to the narrowness of the abortion rights agenda . . . high infant mortality and high maternal mortality rates are just as much a reality for working class women of color as the lack of access to abortion and other health services." Since that time, an expanded agenda by

Black Women's Reproductive History

In her 1997 book, *Killing the Black Body: Race, Reproduction, and the Meaning of Liberty*, Dorothy Roberts talks of the injustices committed against black women throughout history in the area of reproductive rights. She speaks of white slave masters who forced slaves to bear children to work the plantations. She also speaks of more modern policies, such as the thousands of sterilizations without informed consent performed on many southern black women during the 1970s and 1980s.

"Mississippi appendectomies" was the name given to the practice of sterilizing black women without their consent. Sometimes, said Roberts, unnecessary hysterectomies (the surgical removal of the uterus) were performed on poor black women in teaching hospitals. Such a history may be part of the reason that some black women fear abortions.

leading women's organizations goes beyond abortion rights to include issues that are also of great concern to minorities, such as poverty and domestic violence.

Abortion Access for Native Americans

In October 2002, Native American activist Charyn Asetoyer spoke to the U.S. Congress about what she called the dismal state of health care on reservations. Although law requires the Indian Health Service (IHS) to provide abortion services, she cited only twenty-five abortions performed in the past twenty years in IHS facilities. Asetoyer claimed that doctors who work on the reservations tend to be from Catholic countries such as Puerto Rico and are ba-

CECILIA FIRE THUNDER WAS THE FIRST WOMAN PRESIDENT OF THE OGLALA SIOUX TRIBE, AND THE FIRST TO BE IMPEACHED FOR HER PROPOSAL TO OPEN AN ABORTION CLINIC ON THE RESERVATION.

sically opposed to abortions. None of the IHS facilities provide emergency contraception.

After South Dakota announced its new abortion ban in 2006, Cecilia Fire Thunder, president of South Dakota's Oglala Sioux tribe, made news by stating that the Pine Ridge Reservation clinic would provide abortions. Native American reservations are exempt from state law, so the abortion ban did not apply on Pine Ridge. Planned Parenthood, however, said that it did not have the financial resources to open a clinic on the reservation. South Dakota has one of the largest Native American populations of any state.

Religious Attitudes and Policies

Religions all over the world hold different attitudes about abortion. Although the official statements of a church are not always binding on all its members, church leaders and church policies concerning abortion as well as many other issues affect billions of people.

In June 1974, shortly after *Roe v. Wade*, Pope Paul VI issued the Declaration on Procured Abortion, explaining the Catholic Church's antiabortion stand in detail. He wrote: "The tradition of the church has always held that human life must be protected and favored from the beginning, just as at the various stages of its development." In addition, the Church says that "to prevent birth is anticipated murder; it makes little difference whether one destroys a life already born or does away with it in its nascent stage. The one who will be a man is already one."

In 1975, the National Council of Catholic Bishops (NCCB) opposed *Roe v. Wade* with its Pastoral Plan for Pro-Life Activities. This powerful antiabortion force in America urged Congress to pass a law against abortions.

In 1984, a group of priests, nuns, and laypeople called Catholics for a Free Choice ran an ad in the *New York*

Times. The ad stated that Catholics could legitimately hold different views on abortion. It also said that Catholics, including priests and legislators, who disagree with the Church's views should not be penalized by the Church. At the time, Geraldine Ferraro was running for vice president on the Democratic ticket with Walter Mondale. They were defeated by Ronald Reagan and George H. W. Bush. In her speeches, Ferraro, a Catholic, indicated a somewhat mild pro-choice view. That caused John Cardinal O'Connor, Archbishop of New York, to tell Catholics not to vote for her. And that led Catholics for a Free Choice to take out the ad.

Those who signed the statement, including priests, friars, and nuns, received a letter from the head of the Vatican's Sacred Congregation for Religious and Secular Institutes. It said that the ad was "in contradiction to the teachings of the Church." It directed the signers to make a public retraction. It also warned that anyone who did not publicly retract the ad "was to be warned by the superior with an explicit threat of dismissal from his or her religious community."

In March 1995, Pope John Paul II issued the Evangelium Vitae, which means "gospel of life." It condemned three practices: murder of the innocent, abortion, and euthanasia, so-called mercy killing. In the first draft, the pope considered using the word "infallible" concerning Church teachings but decided against it. Infallible would indicate that there is no possibility of error.

More vocal in antiabortion protests are some members of groups known as evangelical Protestants. Some of these protests became violent. "Evangelical" is a term used to describe many denominations with and without the word in the title. It signifies religious groups who believe that salvation comes through personal conversion and following and preaching the scriptures. In all religious groups there is a spectrum of viewpoints on abortion, from total

Religious Attitudes on Abortion

Christian groups

Baptist. The many Baptist denominations in the United States have varied opinions on abortion. The Southern Baptist Convention is the largest Protestant body in the country. Although earlier it generally supported legalized abortions, today it condemns abortion, calling for antiabortion legislation except to save a woman's life. Polls show that most Southern Baptists support legalized abortion. Convention resolutions do not restrict either local churches or individual members.

Catholic. The Roman Catholic Church has about one billion members worldwide, about seventy-eight million in the United States. Individual Catholics differ in their views on abortion, but the Vatican allows abortions in only two cases: ectopic pregnancy, where the embryo grows outside the uterus, and when the uterus is itself cancerous.

Episcopal. Since 1967, abortion is supported under four conditions: rape or incest, a woman's health, a deformed fetus, and an emotional burden. Since 1988, abortion is opposed as a means of birth control or for sex selection.

Lutheran. The American Lutheran Church and the Lutheran Church in America merged into the Evangelical Lutheran Church in America in 1988. It believes that abortion under most conditions is justified. In contrast, the Lutheran Church-Missouri Synod wants a constitutional amendment against abortion that would allow abortion in cases where the pregnancy may mean death for the woman, but not for rape or incest.

Methodist. The official position of the United Methodists, the third largest religious group in the United States, calls for liberal abortion laws. It advocates available contraceptives and supports responsible family planning.

Mormon. The Church of Jesus Christ of Latter-day Saints is strongly against abortion, except in the case of rape or incest. The Reorganized Church of Jesus Christ of Latter-day Saints does not believe that abortion is murder and says a woman has the right to decide whether to terminate the pregnancy.

Orthodox. Both the Greek and Russian Orthodox Churches forbid abortions because they view the fetus as a human being from conception. The Greek Church does allow abortion if the woman's life is in danger. A woman who has an abortion for other reasons, however, is forgiven if she repents; she is not excommunicated.

Pentecostalist. Most, such as the Assemblies of God and the International Pentecostal Church of Christ, are against abortion except in extreme cases when the woman's life is threatened. A much more moderate view is expressed by the Church of the Nazarene and the Church of God (Jerusalem Acres). They do not view abortion as murder and support therapeutic abortions.

Presbyterian. The Presbyterian Church (U.S.A.) has long supported abortion, although it is against late-term abortions or those based on sex selection. Both the Presbyterian Church in America and the Reformed Presbyterian Church of North America strongly condemn abortions.

Unitarian Universalist. Unitarians have long supported legalized abortion.

Hinduism

Abortion is widely practiced in India, even though it is forbidden except for rape or incest. Hindu priests voice few objections, perhaps because of India's huge and rapidly expanding impoverished population.

Islam

This largest single religion in the world—more than one billion people—does not oppose abortion for any reason in the first forty days of pregnancy. There is much difference of opinion, however, among the subgroups. The Koran, Islam's holy book, does not discuss abortion. Use of contraceptives is generally approved among Muslims in America.

Judaism

In general, Jewish law allows abortion when the woman's life and health are threatened. Most Jews support the present U.S. abortion policies. Even the most conservative Orthodox Jews, who reject abortion on demand, recognize it under certain circumstances, such as saving the women's life.

acceptance in all cases by some to total nonacceptance by others. But in the late 1970s and early 1980s, some members of conservative evangelical groups began to put the power of politics into action in spreading their message.

At the time of *Roe v. Wade*, most of these conservative Protestant groups seemed to ignore the decision. Some even supported a woman's right to decide. But by the end of the 1970s, their energy was being focused on abortion and expressing itself through politics. Millions heeded the words of leaders such as Billy Graham and his Christian Action Council, Pat Robertson and his *700 Club*, militant leader Joseph Scheidler, author Francis Schaeffer, Randall Terry of Operation Rescue, and Jerry Falwell, head of the American Coalition for Traditional Values. Some followers of these people went to violent—and illegal—extremes in attempting to sway the public to their beliefs. Throughout this period there were many instances of arson and bombings in abortion clinics, beatings, and even murders of medical personnel who assisted in abortions.

Except for the pope, Billy Graham has been probably the world's best known religious leader for decades. He has been preaching the gospel since 1949. In the 1970s and 1980s, he joined other evangelicals in rallying the faithful against the evils of abortion. So did Pat Robertson, who became the leading religious broadcaster in the country with his *700 Club*. An ordained Southern Baptist minister, he resigned his ordination in 1986 to run—unsuccessfully—for the presidency.

Joseph Scheidler of Chicago united two factions of antiabortion advocates. He joined those who opted for a quiet protest with those who wanted biblical revenge on the people they viewed as sinners. Under Scheidler, these groups joined in antiabortion protests that became militant. Scheidler barnstormed the country praising those who bombed clinics and joining in other acts of harassment against them. He was relentless in his tirades and soon became a national figure for his antics. He led sit-ins at abortion clinics. Once invited to the White House to meet with Ronald Reagan, he asked the president to hold a personal meeting with a man convicted of kidnapping an abortion doctor and bombing clinics. Reagan declined.

Francis Schaeffer united antiabortion advocates in another way. He was already known to evangelical groups when he published *Whatever Happened to the Human Race?* in 1979. It was a pinpoint attack not only against what he called the evil of abortion but also against the United States for the *Roe v. Wade* decision. To Schaeffer, legalized abortion was on the brink of the next step, which he said would be infanticide, or the practice of killing infants. It had to be stopped. The only people who could stop it, said Schaeffer, were Christians who not only believed in the Bible but became political activists. Action was needed.

Schaeffer and his coauthor, C. Everett Koop (later U.S. surgeon general under Reagan), spread their message in a four-month tour of the country in 1979. Evangelical audiences were the target. Schaeffer and Koop are generally credited with motivating people such as Randall Terry.

Terry, a political conservative and religious activist, took Schaeffer's words and put them into action. He founded Operation Rescue in 1987. During the ten years of his leadership, Operation Rescue became the most visible and the most violent of any antiabortion group. In fact, it became so violent that many other evangelical leaders dissociated themselves from Terry and many pro-life organizations claimed that Terry did not represent their principles or their work.

Terry's main targets were abortion clinics. They became the object of picketing, harassing of employees, shouting at would-be patients—and worse. The demon-

THE BATTLE AGAINST ABORTION HAS RESULTED IN VIOLENT DESTRUC-
TION. IN JANUARY 1997, TWO BOMBS WERE DETONATED IN AN
ABORTION CLINIC OUTSIDE ATLANTA, GEORGIA. THE BOMBS WERE
LINKED TO ERIC RUDOLPH, WHO WAS INDICTED FOR THIS, AND OTHER,
CLINIC BOMBINGS.

strators chained themselves to clinic doorways and furniture. Some clinics were set on fire; medical personnel were assaulted. Some clinics were invaded and vandalized. Members of Operation Rescue claimed that such actions—even murder—are justified to save an unborn child. During the Democratic National Convention in Atlanta, Georgia, in 1988, members blockaded a number of abortion clinics in the city. When they were arrested, which they wanted to be, most refused to give their names and were never formally charged with civil disobedience. The group accounted for some seventy thousand arrests nationwide between 1987 and 1994.

Terry himself was arrested more than forty times, the first in 1986 for chaining himself to a sink in an abortion clinic. In 1992, he was sentenced to five months in jail for having a fetus in a jar delivered to Bill Clinton, then the presidential candidate, at the Democratic National Convention. He settled out of court in a 1998 lawsuit brought by NOW, which sought damages for abortion clinics. In that year he also ran unsuccessfully for Congress from New York State.

Jerry Falwell, a Baptist minister, founded the Moral Majority in 1979. This political-action group sought to make values based on the Bible a part of U.S. law. It helped to bring evangelicals into conservative Republican politics just as Ronald Reagan was running for the presidency in 1980. Millions of church members switched parties. Said Pat Robertson after the election, "It was the greatest mass exodus of voters probably in the history of America." The organization was officially disbanded in 1989, but its principles live on in Robertson's Christian Coalition network.

Falwell founded Lynchburg Baptist College, now Liberty University, in Lynchburg, Virginia. Its mission is to join the bible and the U.S. Constitution. A law school was added in 2004. Although ultimately Falwell did not create

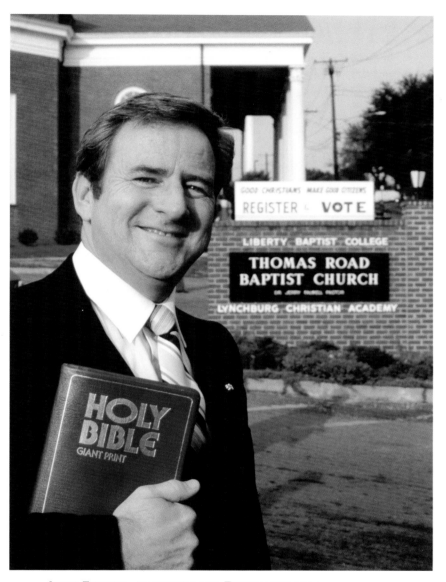

JERRY FALWELL, AN EVANGELICAL BAPTIST AND LEADER OF THE RELI-
GIOUS RIGHT MOVEMENT, HAS LONG BEEN A VOCAL AND POWERFUL
FOE OF ABORTION.

a lasting political movement, he is credited with bringing antiabortion and other conservative beliefs to a mass audience. For years he was the spokesperson for those who believed that abortion was a fundamental wrong in America.

More representative of the mainstream of pro-life organizations are groups such as Concerned Women for America, Americans United for Life, and the Family Research Council. Much of the work of these organizations is centered on disseminating information that outlines their attitudes toward abortion and other issues that concern women and family life. Like the major pro-choice groups, they are also politically active in trying to influence Supreme Court nominations and legislation that favors their cause.

6
Medical Issues

In the mid-nineteenth century, the states began to pass laws that regulated the availability of abortion. But the driving force behind these laws was not so much popular or religious opinion. It was, instead, the organized medical profession. An effective campaign begun by doctors in 1857 and led by Horatio Storer, a specialist in obstetrics and gynecology, focused on the value of human life. The doctors especially spoke of the fetus's right to life. In 1859, at its annual convention, the American Medical Association (AMA) called for an end to legal abortion, including those performed before quickening. Abortion was declared an "unwarranted destruction of human life." Doctors claimed that the rationale behind the declaration was a fear for women's safety. They pointed to the number of poorly qualified personnel and unregistered clinics that were performing abortions at the time. Critics disagreed. They said that by outlawing abortions, doctors protected themselves not only from the loss of patients but also from the loss of revenue that would go to those doctors who performed the abortions.

In 1871, the AMA also denounced doctors who performed abortions. They were called "false to their professions, false to principle, false to honor, false to humanity, false to God." More than a century later, in 1989, the AMA said that abortion was "a 'fundamental right,' to be decided 'free of state interference' in the absence of compelling justification."

In 1951, the American College of Obstetricians and Gynecologists (ACOG) was formed in Chicago, Illinois. This medical specialty narrowed its focus to quality health care for women. With more than forty-nine thousand members today, it is the country's leading professional group providing health care for women. The membership of ACOG, however, is divided on the abortion issue. The American Association of Pro Life Obstetricians and Gynecologists, one of the largest specialty groups within the ACOG, has questioned the pro-choice policy.

Today, physicians are also divided on the issue of abortion. According to its Principles of Medical Ethics, the AMA does not "prohibit a physician from performing an abortion in accordance with good medical practice and under circumstances that do not violate the law." AMA members can decide individually where they stand on abortion. AMA policy encourages its members to become educated on abortion issues and procedures but does not require them to do so.

Most abortions in the United States today are performed by general practitioners. Articles in medical journals have noted that fewer and fewer abortions are performed by obstetrical/gynecological personnel, in many instances because they are not trained or because they fear the violence in certain areas of the country that might result.

Abortion Statistics and Health

Does an abortion affect a woman's health? Most studies show that under proper medical conditions, abortion is

Resident Training Qualifications to Perform Abortions

Family medicine residents are not required to take abortion training, according to the Accreditation Council for Graduate Medical Education (ACGME). Residents can take such training as an elective. Obstetrics and gynecology residents must learn how to handle abortion complications. If the resident is at a religious-affiliated hospital, an alternative site for abortion training must be provided. The ACGME states that its doctors must be able to handle a miscarriage, which is equivalent to handling an abortion in the first trimester.

Not so, say other doctors. According to Dr. Carolyn Westhoff, professor of obstetrics and gynecology at the Columbia University Medical Center in New York: "It [an abortion] is not the same procedure." Commenting on the availability of doctors who perform abortions, she said: "Those who have led abortion care have been physicians at freestanding clinics, not teaching hospitals. The situation hasn't changed much since abortion first became legal, and large medical schools and teaching hospitals have not treated abortion as an important area of training."*

*www.ama-assn.org/amednews/site/free/prsa1024.htm

very safe. The earlier in the pregnancy it is performed, the safer the procedure. About 97 percent of women who have first-trimester abortions have no complications. Some rare serious complications can occur, especially in late-term abortions.

Pro-life advocates point to possible risks in any abortion: surgical risks such as bleeding and infection and possible long-term psychological complications. However, both pro-life and pro-choice groups can cite studies backing their claims that abortion does or does not affect mental health.

Studies seem to indicate that a single abortion does not affect a woman's ability to have healthy children in the future, although less is known about the effects of many abortions or those performed in the second trimester. A low percentage, about 9 percent, of all abortions in the United States take place in the second trimester, or beyond twenty weeks. The two major reasons for these late-term abortions are a medical condition that is discovered to affect a woman's health or a woman not being aware of her pregnancy until the later date. That is more often the case in teenage pregnancies.

According to statistics, most of the women who choose an abortion are under twenty-five years old and unmarried, and about one-third are still in school. The majority are white and are working. The main reasons women give for having an abortion are: (1) having a child would interfere with work or other responsibilities; (2) they cannot afford to have a child; (3) they do not want to raise a child as a single parent.

Medication Abortions

Some women choose medication, as opposed to surgical, abortions, which involve taking a prescription drug. Commonly called medical abortion, the word medication more

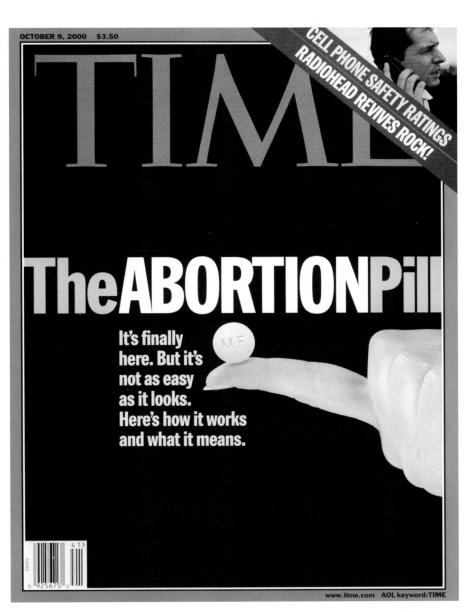

OCTOBER 9, 2000 $3.50

TIME

CELL PHONE SAFETY RATINGS
RADIOHEAD REVIVES ROCK!

TheABORTIONPill

It's finally
here. But it's
not as easy
as it looks.
Here's how it works
and what it means.

M.F

www.time.com AOL keyword:TIME

MIFEPRISTONE (ALSO KNOWN AS RU-486, OR THE "ABORTION PILL")
MADE THE COVER OF *TIME* MAGAZINE ON OCTOBER 9, 2006. THOSE
WHO ARE AGAINST ABORTION BELIEVE THAT IT SHOULD BE ILLEGAL.

accurately describes the procedure, which is a drug-based method of terminating a pregnancy. The medication is usually taken in the doctor's office, and the embryo is expelled much like a miscarriage. A medical abortion is less invasive than surgery. However, if the abortion fails to work, surgery is required.

In 2000, the U.S. Food and Drug Administration (FDA) approved mifepristone for use as an abortifacient. Marketed as RU-486 when it was first produced in France in 1988, it was banned in the United States that same year under the George H. W. Bush administration. Testing began under the Clinton administration in 1992 until its approval by the FDA in 2000.

However, as in all issues concerning abortion, the use of the drug is controversial. Pro-life advocates say it is much more dangerous for women than surgical abortion or bearing the child, claiming the risk of bleeding and infection is great. Furthermore, they say that mifepristone did not go through the usual controls in its FDA study, as do other FDA-approved drugs. Pro-choice advocates believe that mifepristone is safe and that, as another option for women, it will reduce the number of surgical abortions.

As approved by the FDA, mifepristone, taken in pill form, is said to be a safe and effective type of medical abortion. After its approval by the FDA, the drug was made widely available to women across the country. After signing a consent form and making arrangements for surgery in case the medication does not work, the woman takes mifepristone orally in the doctor's office. This is followed two days later by a dose of misoprostol, also by mouth and also approved by the FDA. After this medication has been taken, abortion usually occurs. About two weeks later, the woman visits the doctor's office to make sure that the abortion was successful. If not, she must go to the hospital for surgery.

According to a 2000–2003 study cited by the American Board of Family Practice, medical abortions are more than 95 percent effective. If a medical abortion is not successful, it is followed by surgery. Without surgery, complications such as blood loss may occur.

The Abortion Clinic Then and Now

Before 1973 and the *Roe* v. *Wade* decision, abortions were generally illegal in the United States except in certain areas (New York, for instance, legalized it in 1970) and under certain circumstances, such as approval by therapeutic abortion hospital committees, to save the life of the woman, or in cases of rape or incest. Even where they were illegal, abortions were performed. However, because they were illegal in most places and, therefore, largely unreported, the exact number is unknown. Abortions often took place in out-of-the-way locations, either by unlicensed practitioners or midwives. Sometimes sympathetic doctors performed them at the risk of their medical licenses. It is estimated that during the 1950s and 1960s, for instance, about two hundred thousand to one million illegal abortions took place in the United States. Largely because of the circumstances under which they were done, the death rate was high. In the early 1960s in New York City, for example, 25 percent of childbirth-related deaths among white women were due to abortion. For nonwhites, abortion caused 50 percent of childbirth-related deaths. Before *Roe* v. *Wade*, especially in the 1950s and 1960s, many American women also crossed the border into Mexico for an abortion or traveled to countries in South America or Europe.

The Association to Repeal Abortion Laws (ARAL) was formed in the 1960s by Patricia Maginnis in San Francisco. Along with other advocates of women's rights, she created an underground feminist health agency. ARAL illegally opened pathways for safe abortions to women in need. With ARAL providing a list, thousands of otherwise law-abiding women from all over the United States crossed the border into Mexico. That led to similar agencies such as the Clergy Consultation Service (CCS) in New York. Those who sought help from CCS were first asked to speak to their religious leaders. Soon, other CCS groups sprang up around the country.

In the 1960s, a group of women began what was known simply as JANE in Chicago. They started to refer women seeking abortions to a person they believed to be a doctor in the city. Many women in the group observed the procedures. When the group discovered that the person who performed the abortions was not a doctor at all, the women themselves began to perform abortions over a four-year period. They never turned anyone away for lack of money, and their safety record equaled that of the licensed providers in New York.

The list that ARAL gave to women seeking abortions contained names of and directions for getting to abortion providers, how the procedure would be done, fees, and what preparations the women should make. Although it also listed names in a number of countries, most of the women went to Mexico since it was the easiest to enter.

After *Roe* v. *Wade* in 1973, abortion became a legal option for American women. They could now have abortions in the United States. However, nothing in the Court decision spelled out ways to make these procedures safe and accessible. Catholic hospitals, for instance, did not offer the service, and many women in the United States lived far away from any hospital. Planned Parenthood was one organization that opened safe abortion clinics nationwide. Its models for a safe clinic were those set up in New York City, which had remarkable safety records.

Clinics Face
TRAP Laws

In Albemarle County, Virginia, the Planned Parenthood clinic that opened in 2004 has wider than normal doorways and hallways and bigger than usual patient examination rooms. The staff that runs the clinic says the extra space is defensive; the state might try to pass stricter operating standards by passing a law saying clinics must provide more space. The Virginia clinic feels it is prepared for that possibility.

Virginia is not the only state that may consider TRAP (Targeted Regulation of Abortion Providers) laws. NARAL (National Association for the Repeal of Abortion Laws, which followed ARAL) Pro-Choice America says that thirty-four states have such laws that target abortion providers, but not other medical personnel. The idea, maintains NARAL, is to force the clinics to close, but it is not certain whether TRAP laws have had any effect. However, abortions in Virginia numbered one thousand fewer in 2004 than in the year 2000.

About one million abortions are performed each year in the United States. The large majority are performed in abortion clinics and other nonhospital facilities. That is also true in other countries, such as the Netherlands, Germany, and Poland. Abortions in England and France are performed mainly in hospitals but also in private facilities that are much like American abortion clinics.

In a clinic, abortions are performed on an outpatient basis. This is true for the majority of hospital abortions as well. Only a very small percentage of women are hospitalized overnight, generally because of some medical complication.

The services offered in abortion clinics and hours of operation may differ widely across the country. The city of Yonkers in Westchester County, New York, for instance, has a population of about two hundred thousand. Its Planned Parenthood clinic is open from 9 a.m. to 5 p.m. Monday and Friday, 9 a.m. to 8 p.m. Tuesday through Thursday, and 10 a.m. to 2 p.m. on Saturdays. Women may walk in to seek information on emergency contraception or other issues or to make an appointment for an abortion. The clinic offers many family services. Abortion fees are rated on a sliding scale based on income, family size, and Medicaid and private insurance.

The Planned Parenthood clinic in lower Manhattan claims that protestors are on the sidewalks at least two or three times a week outside its facility. Although the protestors have not been violent, the clinic provides escorts for the women who seek its services.

Abortion clinics became the center of great controversy during the 1988 election when pro-life groups became more visibly aggressive in their campaign to overturn *Roe* v. *Wade*. One of their targets was the abortion clinic. About twenty thousand arrests of those who targeted abortion clinics in nationwide protests occurred in 1989 alone.

Abortions in Secret

When abortion was illegal in the United States, there were reports of so-called abortion mills—hidden, unsanitary places operating in the back alleys and side streets of American cities. If a woman could not afford to go to a country that legalized them, the illegal option might be her only choice. These abortion sites were dangerous, often run by poorly trained people who were not doctors or skilled medical personnel and who were interested only in the money. The abortion sites were often dirty and frightening places.

Then came *Roe v. Wade*. Abortion was legal, and away went the abortion mills . . . but not exactly. An article in the *New York Times* on November 24, 1991, disclosed an abortion mill operating in New York City's Lower East Side. "No one knows how many such fly-by-night surgeries there are in New York City or how many abortions they produce. But law-enforcement officials and medical experts say dozens of these clinics are believed to be tucked away behind storefronts and in more ordinary-looking doctors' offices and they are believed responsible for scores or even hundreds of illegal or incompetent abortions annually."

Who goes to these abortion mills? Usually, they are women who are poor, who perhaps speak little English, and who are unaware of how to find adequate and legal medical treatment. They often have little or no idea of where or how to seek counseling should they need it. They also may be charged whatever the abortion mill demands. The charge may be as little as $150 or as much as $1,500 or more.

The New York State Health Department warned women seeking abortions of such entrapments as abortion mills. In the city, abortions are performed in hospitals, outpatient clinics, licensed physicians' offices, and clinics op-

Violence Task Force

In 1993, during the Clinton administration, the Task Force on Violence Against Abortion Providers was created by the U.S. Justice Department. The aim was to determine if there was a conspiracy among the violators to close the abortion clinics. In mid-1994, the task force was strengthened after a doctor who performed abortions was shot and killed outside a clinic in Pensacola, Florida. This murder was just the latest in a series of murders and/or violence against abortion clinics and their personnel. Activist Paul Hill was convicted of the murder and sentenced to the electric chair. That year, President Bill Clinton signed into law the Freedom of Access to Clinic Entrances (FACE). It became a federal offense to threaten or interfere with clinic personnel or to damage clinic facilities.

Most antiabortion groups vocally condemn violence. Some activists charged that FACE infringes on their freedom of speech. It prohibits force or its threat against anyone providing or getting reproductive services. The Supreme Court indicated there was no infringement by refusing to hear *Woodall* v. *Reno* in June 1995. The refusal thereby upheld the earlier decision of the U.S. Court of Appeals, which ruled that FACE does not infringe on First Amendment rights.

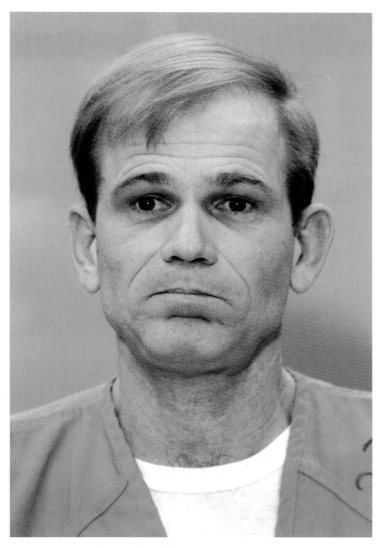

ANTIABORTION ACTIVIST PAUL HILL WAS CONVICTED OF, AND EXECUTED
FOR, THE MURDER OF A DOCTOR AND A BODYGUARD AT AN ABORTION
CLINIC IN PENSACOLA, FLORIDA. HILL BELIEVED HE WAS GOING TO
DEATH AS A MARTYR.

erated by Planned Parenthood. All of them must have emergency backup plans in case of problems with the procedure. New York is one of the few states that covers abortions under Medicaid.

How Other Countries View Abortion

Most countries in the world today have some laws on abortion. Most European nations have generally liberal abortion laws, including predominantly Catholic Italy and Spain. Abortion is illegal mostly in developing countries, where it is a major cause of maternal death. Many developing countries prohibit abortions under any circumstances. However, in practice, the defense that it was necessary to save the life of the woman is usually legally accepted. Many countries allow abortions with so-called significant restrictions, which vary widely. In Muslim countries, the most common restriction is that a woman must have her husband's consent for the procedure. Besides the United States, the countries with the most liberal abortion laws include: Australia, Belgium, Canada, Cuba, Denmark, and North Korea. Those with the most restrictions include Colombia, Egypt, Ireland, Libya, the Philippines, and Venezuela.

In North America, Canada changed from banning all abortions in 1869 to now having some of the world's most liberal policies. The liberalization movement began in the 1960s when a bill allowed abortions to protect a woman's health. However, a three-doctor committee had to approve each procedure. Henry Morgentaler, a Montreal doctor, found the committee to be inconsistent in its rulings, often giving them too late for the abortion to proceed. He began working to change the law. He was sentenced to jail for twenty-eight months, but his work started the fight to reform Canada's abortion laws. Finally, largely through Morgentaler's efforts, the Supreme Court of Canada found Canada's abortion restrictions unconstitutional in 1988.

Canada has abortion upon demand, paid for by the government. About one third of the abortions take place in hospitals, the rest in public and private clinics. Chemical abortion is also available. Since 1988, there have been a few attempts to introduce new limits on the abortion policy, but without success. Canada has one pro-life political party, the Christian Heritage Party of Canada, but none of its members has ever been elected to Parliament.

Latin America and South America have strict limitations on abortion. In Ecuador, for instance, abortion is allowed only in cases of rape if the woman is insane or mentally retarded. Strict limitations generally mean unsafe conditions for the abortions that do take place. In Latin America and the Caribbean, a World Health Organization (WHO) report in 2002 estimated almost one unsafe abortion to every three live births.

In Europe, Russia follows Romania as having the highest abortion rate. For more than half a century, Russia has had a most liberal policy regarding abortions. That may be changing, however. In 2003, a government resolution restricted abortions for the first time since Stalin's ban was lifted in 1955.

Before the resolution, abortions were legal between the twelfth and twenty-second weeks of pregnancy under thirteen circumstances, such as divorce or poverty. Under the new law, the circumstances for abortion have been reduced to four: rape, prison, the husband's death or severe disability, and a court ruling that takes parental rights from the woman.

Some experts say the resolution will not make a marked difference in the Russian abortion rate. But a number of liberals fear that these new restrictions will send

Europe's Human Rights Court Hears Abortion Case

In 2006, a Polish woman who was refused an abortion took her case to the European Court of Human Rights. Pregnant with her fourth child, Alicja Tysiac was warned by three eye specialists that she might go blind if the pregnancy continued.

However, no doctor would authorize terminating the pregnancy. When Poland was under Communist Party rule, abortion was widely available. Today, legislation sponsored by the Catholic Church permits abortions only to save the woman's life, if the fetus is severely damaged, or if the pregnancy occurred from incest or rape. The Court of Human Rights cannot change Poland's abortion laws, but it can decide that Tysiac's rights have been violated.

some women into back-street clinics if they do not fit into the four legal categories of choice.

In 2001, France recognized "the right not to be born." In 1995, a boy was born with severe disabilities: he was deaf, nearly blind, and mentally disabled. The country's highest court of appeal granted compensation ($85,000 in U.S. money) because the doctor did not inform his mother that her pregnancy carried the risk of resulting in a severely disabled child. The mother argued that she was not given the option of an abortion. She is entitled to future payments that may total about $600,000.

That decision and other similar cases caused much debate in France. Attorney-general Jerry Sainte-Rose declared that "The recognition of the concept of a right not to be born is a dangerous one."

Across the developing countries of Africa, often "only wealthy women can afford safe procedures," noted WHO in an article in March 2006. In the same article, Reuters, the international news service, reported: "In Kenya, where abortion is illegal except to save a woman's life, many women are dying after unsafe abortions." About four million abortions are estimated to take place in Africa each year.

Asian countries differ widely in their abortion laws. Since at least the medieval period, abortions were performed extensively in Japan, especially during the late Tokugawa era (1603–1867). But in the late nineteenth century, Japan adopted a penal code much like that of France, a Catholic country. Abortion in Japan was declared a crime. In 1948, following World War II, Japan passed the Eugenic Protection Laws. It made abortions legal to protect the life of the woman and to stop severe birth defects. The law was changed the following year to include so-called economic hardship as a reason for abortions. That virtually opened abortions for any woman.

Abortion became a primary means of birth control in Japan. However, recently the morning-after pill has become available.

Shinto, various sects of Buddhism, and Christianity coexist in Japan. Buddhism is against the practice of abortion. However, its clergy do not take the kind of open stand against the practice that clergy do in the United States.

The history of abortion goes back a long time in China as well. In modern times, attitudes about abortion have more to do with government policy than with religious beliefs. During the Great Leap Forward (1958–1962), Chairman Mao Zedong believed the population was growing too rapidly. Restrictions on abortions were relaxed. In 1979, the government, still alarmed at the expanding population, introduced what it called a short-term measure: the one-child family policy. At the time, China had 25 percent of the world's population and just 7 percent of the world's arable land. The policy was strictly enforced with few exceptions, such as if the first child was born with a disability or the parents were from one-child families. A second child was generally allowed after five years in rural areas, where about 70 percent of the population lived. For success, the policy depended upon contraceptives and abortion.

And the policy generally has worked. The government set 1.2 billion as a population goal by 2000. The census that year ran to 1.27 billion. However, the sex ratio has changed, with a far higher number of male children born. "The picture that emerges is that some urban Chinese make the choice to perform sex selection with the first pregnancy, since they are allowed only one child. In rural areas, most couples are permitted to have a second child, especially if the first is female. So if the second (or subsequent) child is female, the pregnancy often 'disappears,' allowing the couple to have another child in an attempt to have a son," according to an article in worldnetdaily.com.

China watchers feel the one-child family policy may undergo some changes. There is evidence of shifting views about the age-old tradition of preference for boys over girls. One way in which China is trying to redress the preference for male children is by providing girls with more access to schooling and jobs. In addition, the personal freedoms that have come with the economic changes in China make it harder to enforce a male-preference policy.

Abortion was legalized in India in 1971 partly in an attempt to curb the alarming rise in population, especially among the poor. As in China, the policy brought about a marked decline in population, but it also brought other problems, such as the killing of female fetuses. Indian society has long had preferences for the male child. One of the reasons is the practice of a dowry that the parents of the daughter must give to the groom's family upon marriage. A columnist for *The Hindu* newspaper wrote: "The dowry demands today are nothing short of extortion. Many families sell off land and are forced into debt they can never pay off." Conservative estimates say that about ten million female fetuses have been illegally aborted in India over the past twenty years.

Although Indian law says that medical personnel cannot use ultrasound to determine and disclose the sex of the fetus, the law is widely ignored. India's 2001 census showed a drop in the number of girls aged six and under. Says researcher Sabu George: "The future is frightening. Over the next five years we could see more than a million fetuses eliminated every year. At this pace we'll soon have no girls born in the country. We don't know where it will stop."

7
The Politics of Abortion

Most controversies in America involve politics at some point. Abortion is no exception. People on both sides want their views heard. They also, when possible, want their views to become laws. In that way abortion involves not only citizens, but the president, state and federal governments, and the entire court system. As soon as the laws began to change, people began to argue about the changes, and people on all parts of the political spectrum took sides.

The Supreme Court and Abortion Law

Many Americans on either side of the 1973 decision thought that the abortion matter was finally settled. However, in the years following *Roe* v. *Wade*, the Court has taken a number of cases that touch upon some aspect of the issue. Many think the 2006 South Dakota law will eventually wind up there, too. The results of some of the cases presented here show the ways in which the

Court, through the years, has made an impact on earlier decisions as well as the ways in which those decisions are administered.

Harris v. McRae (1980). The Medicaid program was established by Congress in 1965. It gives federal financial assistance to states to cover certain costs of medical treatment for needy persons. In 1976, Congress passed the Hyde Amendment. It denied payment for abortions to those on Medicaid. In 1980, Cora McRae was on Medicaid and pregnant. Medicaid would not pay for an abortion. The Court was asked to decide if the Hyde Amendment was constitutional, or if, among other things, it violated the right to privacy.

On June 30, 1980, the Court, in a 5 to 4 vote, held that the Hyde Amendment was constitutional. Critics said that the decision set up a two-class system of abortion availability. The Court decided that it was not the duty of government to make sure that everyone could afford an abortion.

Thornburgh v. American College of Obstetricians and Gynecologists (1986). A group of doctors, clinics, clergy, and one woman challenged a Pennsylvania state antiabortion law. The law required doctors to tell women seeking abortions about harmful physical and psychological effects. It also imposed detailed record-keeping requirements and mandated that a second doctor be present at the procedure.

The Court struck down most of the provisions, either on invasion of privacy or undue burden. It did not rule on the provision that said requiring minors to get parental consent or a court order for an abortion was an undue burden.

In *The Oxford Companion to the Supreme Court of*

the United States, Hall says: "*Thornburgh* was to be the last case in which a firm majority of the court adhered to the reasoning of *Roe* v. *Wade.* The retirement of Justice Lewis Powell, who had consistently supported *Roe,* and the appointment of Justice Anthony Kennedy led to a substantial assault on the framework established by *Roe* in *Webster* v. *Reproductive Services* (1989)."

Webster v. Reproductive Services (1989). Some case watchers thought this case was evidence of the Court becoming lenient on abortion restrictions. A Missouri law said that life begins at conception and unborn children must be protected. Toward that end, doctors could not perform abortions at state hospitals, nor could state employees or facilities assist in them, nor could anyone in state facilities give a woman advice on getting an abortion. Health care professionals in the state as well as pregnant women seeking abortions filed a class action suit.

By a vote of 5 to 4 the Court overturned the lower court and upheld most of the restrictions, saying they did not violate its earlier abortion decisions. Both sides of the abortion issue saw this as a major change in Court rulings. Pro-life called for state legislatures to pass more restrictions. Pro-choice rounded up their troops by hailing the decision as a threat to the 1973 ruling.

Hodgson v. Minnesota (1990). This was the Court's first confrontation with the abortion issue since *Webster.* A Minnesota statute required minors seeking abortions to tell both parents. It also allowed a minor to obtain an abortion if a court ruled she was mature or that not telling the parents was in her best interests.

The statute had been declared unconstitutional by the district court and reversed by the court of appeals. The Supreme Court upheld the appeals decision 5 to 4 on both

Sandra Day O'Connor Breaks Tradition

Hodgson v. *Minnesota* was the first case in which Justice Sandra Day O'Connor ruled against a restriction on abortion availability. Regarded as part of the conservative wing of the Court, she was the nation's first female justice. Although she generally sided with the conservative members, she also surprised them with her independence. Her opinions tended to narrow the distance between majority and minority votes.

O'Connor changed Court etiquette just by being there. Before her arrival in 1981, members of the Supreme Court were referred to as Mr. Justice. Since then, every member is simply called Justice.

SANDRA DAY O'CONNOR STANDS WITH (THEN VICE PRESIDENT) GEORGE H. W. BUSH IN FRONT OF THE U.S. SENATE AFTER HER UNANIMOUS CONFIRMATION TO THE SUPREME COURT IN 1981. THOUGH GENERALLY CONSERVATIVE, SHE PROVIDED THE SWING VOTE REQUIRED TO KEEP ABORTION LEGAL. SHE RETIRED FROM THE COURT ON JULY 1, 2005.

counts. It said the requirement to tell both parents violated the Constitution. However, it was made constitutional because of the provision for judicial consent. Notes Hall: "The two-parent notification requirement was quite unusual, however, and the implications of *Hodgson* may be quite limited."

Rust* v. *Sullivan (1991). This case involved a statute passed by Congress in 1970. It gave federal funds for family-planning services, but not if abortion was part of the planning. In 1988, under the Reagan administration, the regulations were tightened to include a so-called gag rule. Clinics that got federal funds were no longer allowed to tell pregnant women if abortions were available elsewhere.

Family-planning service providers argued that their rights were violated under the First Amendment and clients' rights were violated as to *Roe* v. *Wade*. In addition, the change in regulations was not authorized by Congress. The Court disagreed and upheld the statute.

Most law watchers found this case to be a clear indication of the Court's shifting views on abortion. Interestingly, one of the attorneys for the government was John Roberts, then principal deputy solicitor general and now chief justice of the U.S. Supreme Court.

Planned Parenthood* v. *Casey (1992). This case is important because, although the Court upheld *Roe* v. *Wade*, it set a new standard to judge restrictive abortion laws. The challenge was against four provisions of the Pennsylvania Abortion Control Act of 1982.

The plaintiffs were five abortion clinics and a class action group of physicians who provided the services. The law required a twenty-four-hour waiting period for an abortion; doctors to give women information about health risks and possible complications; minors to have the consent of parents or guardian before receiving an abortion; and women to inform their husbands before the procedure, the so-called spousal notification.

In a bitter 5 to 4 decision, the Court found all but one of the Pennsylvania laws constitutional. It said that informing the spouse was an undue burden on the woman's right to have an abortion but that the other requirements were not. Court watchers noted that, although the majority opinion upheld the right to an abortion, it lowered the standard for analyzing restrictions on that right.

Abortion and the Presidency

The office of president of the United States is the most powerful position in the nation as well as the world. When presidents voice their views, it's big news. It also sways a lot of potential voters. Especially since *Roe* v. *Wade*, presidential candidates have been asked where they stand on abortion.

One of the president's major areas of power rests with his constitutional authority to nominate justices to the Supreme Court. The Senate, however, must approve the president's nominations. That does not always happen, but it occurs often enough to make presidents highly influential in changing U.S. law. Through the years, the fate of abortion laws has generally rested with the makeup of the Court.

Roe v. *Wade* became law during the second term of Republican Richard M. Nixon (1969–1974). He appointed Warren E. Burger to serve as chief justice. Generally viewed as a conservative, Burger often edged to the moderate side. He concurred with the majority opinion on *Roe* v. *Wade*. Nixon also appointed Harry A. Blackmun and Lewis F. Powell Jr. Blackmun was thought to be conservative when he joined the Court, but in time his views moved toward the liberal side. Powell generally voted conservative but not when it came to *Roe v. Wade*. Nixon did get a true conservative when he nominated William H. Rehnquist, one of the dissenters.

Gerald Ford (1974–1977) succeeded Nixon, who was forced to resign because of the Watergate scandal. Abortion was now legal. Jimmy Carter (1977–1981) made no appointments to the Court. Ronald Reagan (1981–1989) rode the crest of religious conservatism sweeping the country. However, he did nominate Sandra Day O'Connor, the first woman to be Supreme Court justice.

The administration of George H. W. Bush (1989–1993) is on record as committed to pro-life. It demonstrated that by filing briefs in support of the antiabortion law in *Planned Parenthood* v. *Casey*. But most important to pro-life supporters were Bush's nominations to the Court. Shortly after the Court, led by conservative Chief Justice Rehnquist, handed down its lenient restriction decision in *Webster*, Bush named another conservative, David Souter, who declined to voice his opinion on legalized abortion. Within a year, Bush had the chance for another nomination when Thurgood Marshall retired. In came a young black conservative, Clarence Thomas. The appointment was controversial mainly because Anita Hill, a law professor and his former employee, accused Thomas of sexual harassment. He was voted to the Court by the smallest margin of approval, 52 to 48, in more than one hundred years.

Bush was followed by Democrat Bill Clinton (1993–2001). A liberal on abortion law, Clinton nominated two justices, Ruth Bader Ginsburg and Stephen Breyer, both considered moderates. But when George W. Bush took office in 2002, a conservative was back in power. Bush, who makes no secret of his antiabortion stance, has tried to keep the Court conservative with the nominations of John Roberts as chief justice and Samuel Alito as associate justice.

NEWLY APPOINTED SUPREME COURT CHIEF JUSTICE JOHN ROBERTS (R) STANDS WITH PRESIDENT GEORGE W. BUSH AND THE ARCHBISHOP OF WASHINGTON ON THE STEPS OF ST. MATTHEW'S CATHEDRAL. ROBERTS IS EXPECTED TO VOTE WITH THE ANTIABORTION WING OF THE COURT.

National Politics and Abortion

It is the work of the U.S. Congress to pass laws that influence and regulate the day-to-day lives of Americans. And even though abortion is legal, Congress can infringe upon or expand the laws to make abortion less or more accessible. That occurred when the first major congressional legislation that concerned abortion after *Roe v. Wade* was passed. Congress banned the spending of federal Medicaid funds for abortion in 1976. There have been similar bans ever since.

In 1977, Congress ruled that employers did not have to pay health insurance benefits for abortions unless the woman's life was in danger (Pregnancy Disability Amendment of 1977 to Title VII of 1964 Civil Rights Act). The appropriations bill for the Department of Defense in 1982 meant that women in the military could not get abortions in military hospitals.

A bill passed by the U.S. Senate in July 2006 concerned minors and abortion. The Senate bill makes it a crime for anyone to take a pregnant minor across a state line for an abortion in order to evade telling the parents.

Once again, the bill divided people. Its backers said it protects young girls from a predatory male who wants to arrange a secret abortion to cover up the pregnancy. Minors need a parent's okay just to get an aspirin from the school nurse, they said; why should abortion be different? But critics believed that the bill would harm victims of abuse and/or incest. "I think it will make them fearful," said Senator Barbara Boxer, Democrat from California. "I think it will make them feel alone." The National Right to Life Committee claimed the bill would stop the widespread breaking of notification laws. Pro-choice groups called it the Teen Endangerment Act.

More Danger
for Girls?

In an article in the *New York Times* on August 6, 2006, a woman tells of her experiences helping teenagers from out-of-state get later-term abortions in New York, where they are legal through the twenty-fourth week. Typically, she says, the girls are minors. Abortions in their own states were delayed because of such laws requiring parent notification and waiting periods, and Medicaid restrictions. She says that the Senate bill will put already at-risk girls in greater danger. She also claims that the bill cannot protect the minor whose parents are missing or abusive.

Studies say that about 60 percent of minors who get abortions do tell one or both parents. The other 40 percent don't do so for good reasons, such as incest or violence in the family.

Before it becomes law, the Senate bill must be joined with the version passed by the House on September 26, 2006. President Bush said he will sign it. Anyone, even a grandmother or other relative, who helps a minor cross a state line can be fined and face a year in prison.

Abortion and the States

In the late 1960s and early 1970s, there was increasing pressure on state legislatures to liberalize restrictive abortion laws. At the time only four states—Alaska, Hawaii, New York, and Washington, plus the District of Columbia —allowed an abortion for any reason. Three states— Louisiana, New Hampshire, and Pennsylvania—denied all abortions. Mississippi allowed it only in rape cases and to save a woman's life. Thirteen states allowed abortions to protect a woman's physical and mental health (Arkansas, California, Colorado, Delaware, Florida, Georgia, Kansas, Maryland, New Mexico, North Carolina, Oregon, South Carolina, and Virginia). The remaining twenty-nine states permitted abortions only to save a woman's life.

After *Roe v. Wade*, state legislatures faced a new pressure as pro-life and religious groups wanted restrictions on the abortion laws. Since 1973, state laws set up continuing challenges to the Supreme Court decision. The latest restriction was the South Dakota ban on abortions in that state, which the state's voters rejected in November 2006. In truth, the ruling in *Roe v. Wade* did give the state legislatures wiggle room for some limitations. Those that are against the Court's decision hope that in time the wiggle room will allow state laws that will eventually cause the overturn of *Roe v. Wade*.

At present, *Roe v. Wade* and other decisions of the Court limit state restrictions on abortion to four general categories:

115

1. Informed consent. A state may require that a woman seeking an abortion must be given information about the procedure as well as any alternatives, such as a state program to help her care for the baby.

2. Parental consent. States may require permission from one or both parents if the girl is under age eighteen. In those states, the High Court says the girl must also be given the option of getting consent from a judge instead of the parents.

3. Parental notice. Some states say that the parents have to be told about an abortion, but that consent is not required. The Court's option also applies here.

4. Viability. Some states refuse abortions after the time when the fetus could survive outside the womb.

In addition to the restrictions in the four general categories, the states have laws that do not prevent a woman from getting an abortion but do specify under what conditions. Some may appear to conflict with the Court decision but have not yet been challenged.

Most states (thirty-eight) require an abortion to be performed by a qualified physician, and twenty states say the procedure must be done in a hospital. Some states (twenty-four) say the woman must wait for a specified period before an abortion, usually twenty-four hours. Both Rhode Island and Tennessee have laws against nonsurgical, or medication, abortions. California, Michigan, New Mexico, and Pennsylvania passed laws outlawing violence against abortion clinics. Forty-six states allow certain

State Restrictions
on Abortion*

1 = informed consent; 2 = parental consent; 3 = parental notice; 4 = viability. Details vary within the states.

AK	2 (no court option)	MN	3
AL	2	MO	2, 4
AR	3	MS	1, 2
AZ	2	MT	3
CA	2	NC	2
CO	2 (no court option)	ND	2
DE	3	NE	3
GA	3	NM	2 (no court option)
IA	3	NV	3
ID	3 (no court option)	OH	1, 3, 4
IL	3	PA	1, 2, 4
IN	1, 2	RI	2
KS	3	SC	2
KY	2	SD	1, 3 (no court option)
LA	1, 2	TN	2
MA	2, 3	UT	1, 3 (no court option)
MD	3 (abortion provider decides whether to notify parents)	WI	1, 2
		WV	3
		WY	2
MI	1, 2		

*These thirteen states have no restrictions:
CT, FL, HI, ME, NH, NJ, NY, OK, OR, TX, VA, WA

medical personnel to refuse to participate in abortion procedures for reasons of religion or conscience. Only Missouri prohibits all public employees from participating in abortions.

States adopt licensing and reporting requirements for abortions, such as that they must be performed in licensed hospitals or clinics. In most states with that requirement, those who perform abortions must report them to the public health authorities. However, the Court has judged some of these requirements illegal. In *Planned Parenthood Association of Kansas City, Missouri* v. *Ashcroft*, the Court struck down a state law that said abortions after twelve weeks must be performed in a hospital.

In some states advertising about abortion services was banned before *Roe*, even if abortions took place outside the state. In 1975 *Bigelow* v. *Virginia* went before the Supreme Court. Jeffrey Bigelow, editor of *Virginia Weekly* in Charlottesville, was sued for breaking a state statute that made it illegal to publish anything that encouraged abortion. His publication carried an advertisement for the Women's Pavilion, a nonprofit group that helped women get abortions in New York City. The Court ruled 7 to 2 that the state law violated free speech rights under the First Amendment.

A major restriction in obtaining abortions is money, especially for many women who are poor, many of whom are people of color. One way for states to limit abortion availability is simply to deny state funds to pay for them or to prohibit them from taking place in state hospitals, which many do. In several cases, the Court basically decided that a woman does have the right to decide on an abortion, but that state governments do not have to pay for it.

Decades after the *Roe* v. *Wade* decision, the debate goes on. Pro-choice people debate pro-life people. The federal government keeps an eye on state restrictions. The Supreme Court keeps an eye on both.

Will the Issue Ever Be Settled?

At least in the foreseeable future, it is unlikely that disagreements over abortion will end. Abortion will be a subject of controversy as long as there are unwanted pregnancies. It will be an issue as long as unwed teenagers and victims of rape and incest become pregnant, or fetuses are severely malformed through drugs, genetics, or injury. Abortion will be a political and personal fight as long as embryos offer a hope for curing disease and deformity. For some people, abortion will never be the answer to any of these conditions. For others, it may be the only answer.

It is unrealistic to expect that those on either side of the abortion controversy will change their minds. But there is hope that in a democratic society, the two sides can discuss their feelings and fears without violence and threats. As long as abortion is a legalized procedure in the United States, the facilities that offer the service must be free of violence and harm. All but the most militant of antiabortion groups agree on that.

There may even be other areas of possible agreement between the two sides. Both pro-choice and pro-life advocates want to see fewer pregnancies among unwed teens, for instance. Can the leading organizations for both sides come together in an effort to provide better information to minors—and all women—on reproduction and reproductive services?

Pro-choice advocates are fighting to keep legalized abortion legal. Pro-life advocates are fighting for the overturn of *Roe* v. *Wade* and making sure all abortion becomes illegal. If the ruling were overturned, the right to an abortion would be left to the states. At present, sixteen states,

Abortions Guaranteed by State Constitution or Statute

Sixteen U.S. states presently guarantee a woman's right to an abortion in the state constitution or by statute. They are: Arkansas, California, Connecticut, Florida, Hawaii, Maine, Maryland, Massachusetts, Minnesota, Montana, Nevada, New Jersey, New Mexico, Tennessee, Washington, and West Virginia.

either in their constitutions or by statute, guarantee a woman's right to an abortion. The remaining states would have to pass some type of freedom of choice act to keep abortions legal were the Court to overturn its 1973 decision. In that event, doctors and anyone else who aided a woman in an abortion would probably be subject to long prison terms.

Studies show that a majority of the American public believe that abortions should remain a legal choice with some restrictions. But no matter what happens in the future, abortion is not going to disappear. Laws do not stop abortions.

Perhaps the most important goal at present is for pro-choice and pro-life advocates, and all the organizations that back them, to come together to discuss these topics calmly, reasonably, and without malice or violence. That would be a giant step toward an understanding of the issue that continues to divide us.

Notes

Foreword

p. 7, par. 4, http://news.bbc.co.uk (accessed March 7, 2006).

p. 7, par. 4, http://www.washingtonpost.com (accessed February 23, 2006).

p. 9, par. 1, http://news.bb.co.uk (accessed March 7, 2006).

p. 9, par. 4, http://www.washingtonpost.com (accessed February 23, 2006).

Chapter 1

p. 12, par. 1, Alexander Sanger, *Beyond Choice* (New York: Public Affairs, 2004) 23.

p. 12, par. 4, R. Sauer, "Attitudes to Abortion in America, 1800–1973," *Population Studies* 28:1 (March 1974): 58.

p. 16, par. 4, Barbara Hinkson Craig and David M. O'Brien, *Abortion and American Politics* (Chatham, NJ: Chatham House, 1993) 5.

p. 20, par. 5, p. 22, par. 1, Kermit L. Hall, *The Oxford Companion to the Supreme Court of the United States* (New York: Oxford University Press, 1992) 3.

p. 22, par. 3, Janet Hadley, *Abortion: Between Freedom and Necessity* (Philadelphia: Temple, 1996) 2.

Chapter 2

p. 30, par. 3, Paul Campos, "Abortion and the Rule of Law," *Scripps Howard News Service*, January 2002, 1.

p. 30, par. 4, Kenneth Cauthen, "The Abortion Debate," May 30, 2006, http://www.users.ox.ac.uk/~mert2049/philoso-phyblairpolitics_ofabortion.sthml, 1 (accessed May 30, 2006).

p. 30, par. 5–p. 31, par. 1, President Ronald Reagan, "Abortion and the Conscience of the Nation," *The Human Review*, Spring 1983, http://www.nationalreview.com (accessed June 1, 2006).

p. 31, par 2, Hadley, *Abortion*, 78.

p. 42, par. 3, Rick Weiss, "Harvard Begins Private Stem-Cell Research Project," *Journal News*, June 7, 2006, 8B.

Chapter 3

p. 43, par. 2–p. 44, par. 1, Nancy E. Adler, et al., "Abortion Among Adolescents," *American Psychologist* (March 2003): 58(3), p. 212.

p. 49, par. 2, Adam Liptak, "Prisons Often Shackle Pregnant Inmates in Labor," *New York Times*, March 2, 2006, p. A1.

p. 49, par. 3, Liptak, *New York Times*.

p. 50, par. 3, http://www.abcnews.go.com/USCenter/wireStory ?id, October 14, 2005. (accessed May 30, 2000.)

p. 51, par. 3, "Partial-Birth Abortion Ban Act," http://en.wikipedia.org/wiki/Partial-Birth_Abortion_Ban_Act (accessed June 4, 2006).

Chapter 4

p. 61, par. 3, *Fact Sheet: Women's Health Policy Facts* (accessed March 2006).

p. 61, par. 4, "Obstructing Access to Emergency Contraceptives in Hospital Emergency Rooms," http://www.planned-parenthood.org/news-articles-press/politics-policy-issues/birth (accessed October 20, 2006).

p. 62, par. 3, Molly M. Glinty, "Some Hospitals Withhold Plan B After Rape," http://www.womensenews.org/article.cfm/dyn/aid (accessed December 27, 2005).

p. 62, par. 4–p. 63, par. 1, Glinty, "Some Hospitals."

p. 66, par. 2, "US Pharmacists Battle over Forced Dispensation of Abortion Drugs," http://www.lifesite.net/ldn/2005/apr/05041504.htm (accessed June 6, 2006).

p. 66, par. 2, "US Pharmacists."

Chapter 5

p. 70, par. 2–p. 71, par. 1, Cassie M. Chew, "Black Women Shape Their Own Message at March for Women's Lives," *Crisis* 111:4 (Jul/Aug 2004): 14–15.

p. 71, par. 3, Rashmi Luthra, "Toward a Reconceptualization of 'Choice': Challenges by Women at the Margins," *Feminist Issues* 12:1 (Spring 1993): 41–54.

p. 74, par. 5, Catholic Library: Declaration on Procured Abortion, http://www.newadvent.org/library/docs_df75ab.htm (accessed April 14, 2006).

p. 75, par. 2, Catholics and Abortion: Authority vs. Dissent, http://www.religion-online.org/showarticle.asp?title=1926. (accessed April 14, 2006).

p. 82, par. 3, James Risen and Judy L. Thomas, *Wrath of Angels: The American Abortion War* (New York: Basic Books, 1998) 130.

Chapter 6

p. 85, par. 1, Physiciansforlife.org/content/view, 521/26 (accessed October 24, 2006).

p. 85, par. 2–p. 86, par. 1, Physiciansforlife. (accessed June 2006).

p. 86, par. 3, Physiciansforlife.

p. 95, par. 2, Robert D. McFadden, "Abortion Mills: Thriving Behind Secrecy and Fear," *New York Times*, November, 24, 1991: 1.

p. 101, par. 4, Wim Weber, "France's Highest Court Recognizes 'The Right Not To Be Born,'" *Lancet*, 358:9297 (12/8/2001):1972.

p. 101, par 3, Weber, "France's Highest Court."

p. 101, par. 4, "Hemorrhage, Hypertension Leading Cause of Maternal Death in Developing Countries, WHO report says," http://www.medicalnewstoday.com/medicalnews.php?newsid=40518 (accessed October 28, 2006).

p. 102, par. 4, "The Effect of China's One-Child Family Policy after 25 Years," *New England Journal of Medicine*, http://content.nejm.org/cgi/content/full/353/11/1171 (accessed March 2006).

p. 103, par. 2, "10 Million Females Illegally Aborted in India," *WorldNet Daily*, http://www.worldnetdaily.com/news/

article/asp?article_id=50947.

p. 103, par 2, "10 Million Females."

Chapter 7

p. 105 par. 6–p. 106, par. 1, Hall, *Oxford Companion*, 872.

p. 109, par. 1, Hall, 405.

p. 113, par. 3, "Senate Backs Curb on Minors' Travel for Abortion," http://www.washingtonpost.com/wp-dyn/con tent/article/2006/07/25/AR2006072501127.html (accessed June 12, 2006).

Further Information

Books

Boston Women's Health Book Collective. *Our Bodies, Ourselves*. New York: Simon & Schuster, 2005.

Brownmiller, Susan. *Against Our Will: Men, Women and Rape*. New York: Bantam, 1986.

Gottfried, Ted. *Teen Fathers Today*. New York: 21st Century, 2000.

Heller, Tania. *Pregnant! What Can I Do!* Jefferson, NC: McFarland, 2002.

Ponton, Lynn. *The Romance of Risk: Why Teenagers Do the Things They Do*. New York: Basic Books, 1998.

Powers, Meghan. *The Abortion Rights Movement*. Detroit: Thomson, 2006.

Web Sites

Pro-Choice/Pro-Life Organizations
These are a few of the many pro-choice and pro-life organizations throughout the country. Most of the larger groups have local chapters.

Pro-Choice
Catholics for a Free Choice
1436 U Street NW, Suite 301
Washington, DC 20009-3997
http://www.catholicsforchoice.org
Dedicated to helping men and women make sound decisions

Center for Reproductive Rights
120 Wall Front Street
New York, NY 10005
http://www.CRLP.org
info@reprorights.org
Concerned with freedom of reproductive rights worldwide

Family Health International
P.O. Box 13950
Research Triangle Park, NC 27709
http://www@fhi.org
Dedicated to the health of families throughout the world

NARAL Pro-Choice America (formerly National Abortion and Reproductive Rights Action League)
1156 15th Street NW, Suite 700
Washington, DC 20005
http://www.prochoiceamer.org
Since 1969, dedicated to women's health and freedom of choice

Planned Parenthood Federation of America (PPFA)
810 Seventh Avenue
New York, NY 10019-5882
http://www.plannedparenthood.org
One of the nation's largest and most active organizations for health services

Religious Coalition for Reproductive Choice
1025 Vermont Avenue NW, Suite 1130
Washington, DC 20005
http://www.RCRC.org
Info.rcrc.org
Pro-faith, pro-family, pro-choice

Pro-Life
American Life League
Box 1350
Stafford, VA 22555
http://www@all.org
Coordinates a network of local groups dedicated to the sacredness of human life

Americans United for Life
310 S. Peoria, Suite 300
Chicago, IL 60607
http://www.unitedforlife.org
Info@AUL.org
Defends human life through law and education

Heartbeat International
665 E. Dublin-Granville Road, Suite 440
Columbus, OH 43229
http://www.pregnancycenters.org
Largest group of pro-life pregnancy centers in the world

National Right to Life Committee (NRLC)
512 10th Street NW
Washington, DC 20004
http://www.nrlc.org
Nation's largest pro-life group, opposed to abortion, euthanasia, and infanticide; more than 3,000 chapters

Republican National Coalition for Life
Box 618
Alton, IL 62002
http://rnclife.org
Founded by Phyllis Schlafly in 1990 to maintain Republican Party's commitment to pro-life principles

Bibliography

Books

Blanchard, Dallas A. *The Anti-Abortion Movement and the Rise of the Religious Right*. New York: Twayne, 1994.

———, and Terry J. Prewitt. *Religious Violence and Abortion: The Gideon Project*. Gainesville: University Press of Florida, 1993.

Brodie, Janet Farrell. *Contraception and Abortion in 19th Century America*. Ithaca, NY: Cornell University Press, 1994.

Butler, J. Douglas and David F. Walbert. *Abortion, Medicine, and the Law*. New York: Facts on File, 1992.

Craig, Barbara Hinkson, and David M. O'Brien. *Abortion and American Politics*. Chatham, NJ: Chatham House, 1993.

Davis, Nanette J. *From Crime to Choice: The Transformation of Abortion in America*. Westport, CT: Greenwood, 1985.

Gorney, Cynthia. *Articles of Faith: A Frontline History of the Abortion Wars*. New York: Simon & Schuster, 1998.

Hadley, Janet. *Abortion: Between Freedom and Necessity*. Philadelphia: Temple, 1996.

Hall, Kermit L., ed. *The Oxford Companion to the Supreme Court of the United States*. New York: Oxford University Press, 1992.

Harrison, Maureen, and Steve Gilbert, eds. *Abortion Decisions of the United States Supreme Court: The 1990's*. Beverly Hills, CA: Excellent Books, 1993.

O'Connor, Karen. *No Neutral Ground? Abortion Politics in an Age of Absolutes*. New York: Westview, 1996.

Risen, James, and Judy L. Thomas. *Wrath of Angels: The American Abortion War*. New York: Basic Books, 1998.

Rudy, Kathy. *Beyond Pro Life and Pro Choice*. Boston: Beacon, 1996.

Sanger, Alexander. *Beyond Choice*. New York: Public Affairs, 2004.

Sloan, Don, M.D., with Paula Hartz. *Abortion: A Doctor's Perspective/A Woman's Dilemma*. New York: Donald I. Fine, 1992.

Solinger, Rickie. *Abortion Wars: A Half Century of Struggle, 1950–2000*. Berkeley: University of California Press, 1998.

Thornhill, Randy, and Craig T. Palmer. *A Natural History of Rape*. Cambridge, MA: MIT, 2000.

Tushnet, Mark. *Constitutional Issues: Abortion*. New York: Facts on File, 1996.

Weddington, Sarah. *Question of Choice: The Lawyer Who Won Roe v. Wade*. New York: Putnam, 1992.

Articles

Adler, Nancy E., et al. "Abortion Among Adolescents," *American Psychologist* 58:3 (March 2003): 211–217.

"Alternatives to the Pill for Contraception," www.fertility-weekly.com, May 9, 2005.

Chew, Cassie M. "Black Women Shape Their Own Message at March for Women's Lives," *Crisis* 111:4 (Jul/Aug 2004): 14–15.

Cook, Rebecca J., Bernard M. Dickens, and Laura E. Bliss. "International Developments in Abortion Law from 1988 to 1998," *American Journal of Public Health* 89:4: 579–586.

Cunningham, Gregg L. "Wave of the Future?" *National Review* (November 10, 1997): 36–38.

Dore, Hollander. "Pregnancies among Rape Victims," *Family Planning Perspectives* 28:6 (Nov/Dec 1996): 244.

Dugger, Karen. "Race Differences in the Determinants of Support for Legalized Abortion," *Social Science Quarterly* 72:3 (September 1991).

Feminist Studies 30:2, "Do Prisoners Have Abortion Rights?" (Summer 2004): 353–381.

Grossman, Richard A., and Bryan D. Grossman. "How Frequently Is Emergency Contraception Prescribed?" *Family Planning Perspectives* 26:6 (Nov/Dec 1994): 270.

Hevesi, Dennis. "Abortion Doctor Is Accused of Using Dirty Tools," *New York Times*, December 18, 1991.

Kalist, David E., "Abortion and Female Labor Force Participation: Evidence Prior to *Roe v. Wade*," *Journal of Labor Research* XXV:3 (Summer 2004).

LII/Legal Information Institute, "Supreme Court Collection: Roe v. Wade (No. 70–18)," Cornell Law School (February 24, 2006).

McFadden, Robert D. "Abortion Mills Thriving Behind Secrecy and Fear," *New York Times*, November 24, 1991.

Meehan, Mary. "*ACLU v. Unborn Children*," *Human Life Review* 27:2 (Spring 2001): 49.

Mooney, Christopher Z., and Lee Mei-Hsien. "Legislative Morality in the American States: The Case of Pre-Roe Abortion Regulation Reform," *American Journal of Political Science* 39:3 (August 1995): 599–627.

Parfitt, Tom. "Russia moves to curb abortion rates," *Lancet* 362:9388 (September 20, 2003): 968.

Perez-Pena, Richard. "East Village Doctor Convicted of Performing Illegal Abortion," *New York Times*, February 23, 1993.

Reagan, Leslie J. "Crossing the Border for Abortions: California Activists, Mexican Clinics, and the Creation of a Feminist Health Agency in the 1960s," *Feminist Studies* 26:2 (Summer 2000): 323–348.

Rodman, Hyman. "Should Parental Involvement Be Required for Minors' Abortions? *Family Relations* 40:2 (April 1991): 155–160.

Sauer, R. "Attitudes to Abortion in America, 1800–1973." *Population Studies* 28:1 (March 1974): 53–67.

Smith, Andrea. "Beyond Pro-Choice Versus Pro-Life: Women of Color and Reproductive Justice," *NWSA Journal* 17:1 (Spring 2005).

Smugar, Steven S., Bernadette Spina, and Jon F. Metz. "Informed Consent for Emergency Contraception: Variability in Hospital Care of Rape Victims," *American Journal of Public Health* 90:9 (September 2000): 1372.

Sperling, Daniel. "Maternal Brain Death," *American Journal of Law & Medicine* (2004): 453–500.

Teo, Wesley D. "Abortion: The Husband's Constitutional Rights," *Ethics* 85:4 (July 1975): 337–342.

"US pharmacies vow to withhold emergency contraception," www.thelancet.com, vol. 365, May 14, 2005.

Weber, Wim, "France's highest court recognizes 'the right not to be born,'" *Lancet* 358:9297 (December 8, 2001): 1972.

Index

Page numbers in **boldface** are illustrations, tables, and charts.

REDMOND HIGH SCHOOL LIBRARY